DISCARD

D1119940

GREAT
INDIAN
FEASTS

Mridula Baljekar

GREAT INDIAN FEASTS

130 wonderful, simple recipes
for every festive occasion

JB

JOHN BLAKE

Published by John Blake Publishing Ltd,
3, Bramber Court, 2 Bramber Road,
London W14 9PB, England

www.blake.co.uk

First published in Hardback in 2005

ISBN 1 84454 141 X

British Library Cataloguing-in-Publication Data:

A catalogue record for this book is available from the
British Library.

Design by www.envydesign.co.uk

Printed in Spain by Bookprint, S.L., Barcelona

1 3 5 7 9 10 8 6 4 2

Papers used by John Blake Publishing are natural,
recyclable products made from wood grown in sustainable
forests. The manufacturing processes conform to the
environmental regulations of the country of origin.

With love for my daughters,
Maneesha and Sneha

Acknowledgements

There are many people I have to thank who have helped, supported and encouraged me in compiling this unique book. I have listed the names below, but if I have missed anyone, it is definitely not intentional!

First and foremost, my thanks to Schwartz for supplying me with their wonderful range of spices which I have used in all my recipes in this book.

Special thanks to Cobra Beer for their continued support.

My sincere thanks to Joseph Chandy for his all-round help and support.

Susan Flynn for her enthusiastic PR support.

John Salway, the excellent butcher who supplies my restaurant, for providing me with top-quality meat and poultry at short notice while I was testing the recipes for this book.

With thanks to Matt Munro for the photography, my food stylist Jane Suthering and prop stylist Penny Markham.

Last, but not least, a big thank you to the following members of the Spice Route team who undertook all the chores of shopping and helping to prepare ingredients during photography:

Srinivasa Reddy Vuyyuru
Neeraj Saraswat
Vijay Singh Negi
Narpat Shekhawat

I am grateful to the author Om Lata Bahadur for her book *The Book of Hindu Festivals and Ceremonies*, which has been an immense source of information.

vii

Mridula Baljekar

Introduction

I would like to invite you to follow me on a trail of great feasts based on festivals and celebrations across India. During your journey through the spice-laden route of Indian festivals, you will encounter some really special recipes which you can use for any kind of celebration. I have simplified these recipes to suit today's busy cooks, of which I am one! There is also a wide selection of really simple festival recipes which are just as suitable for everyday use.

There are 13 major festivals in India in 12 months! I have compiled brief introductions with recipes for most of the major ones. As I am a believer in mixing tradition with innovation, I have also included recipes for Christmas and Easter with an Indian twist which have been a great success in my restaurant, Spice Route in Windsor.

During festivals, food is the focal point. Festivals are times of togetherness, of sharing the common ground provided by religious and social beliefs, and of guiding the younger generation towards caring and sharing.

The essence of India can easily be equated to diversity. The diverse nature of the country is evident in its varied geographical and climatic conditions, range of religious faiths, innumerable languages spoken and its variety of architectural monuments such as Christian churches, Muslim mosques and Hindu temples. India is a place where one also comes across renaissance and baroque, terracotta and brick, the hustle and bustle of modern living, and serene tranquillity, where one day stretches languidly into the next.

Over the centuries, with tremendous grace and generosity, India absorbed the many different religions and cultures that it encountered, cleverly integrating them into the already colourful history and civilisation of the country. Every religion and each community belonging to different religious and cultural sectors has its own distinct food ethos, most of which are believed to have been influenced by the Aryans, who were the first invaders to enter India. They saw food as possessing a higher moral significance as well as nourishing the body. Over time, the Aryan religion became the foundation of the single most indigenous faith, Hinduism. Thus, the ethos of Hindu festival foods, influenced by the Aryan beliefs, became firmly established in the country.

Upanishad, one of India's holy scriptures, states, 'From food are all creatures produced, by food do they grow. The self consists of food, of breath, of mind, of understanding, of bliss.'[1] Another holy

1 *Indian Food – A Historical Companion* by K T Achaya

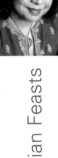

Great Indian Feasts

scripture, the Bhagavad Gita, states, 'From food do all creatures come into being.'

From Hinduism evolved Buddhism, Jainism and Sikhism. They have common elements with the ethos of Hindu festival foods, but also display distinctive features of their own. Islam and Christianity came to India much later. Obviously, they have their own festival foods according to their respective religions. All these religious factors have created a dazzling variety of festival foods in India. Each festival in each religion has its own particular kind of food associated with the season and the crops. It is also customary to cook and serve certain types of food items during each festival. This practice is based on Hindu mythology. The Hindu religion believes in more than one god and goddess. Each god or goddess is believed to be the patron of a particular profession or trade. For instance, a farmer would worship the Sun God and the God of Rain. Each of these gods is supposed to have his particular favourite dish. The farmer would prepare these dishes so that the gods might look favourably on him and bless him with a fruitful harvest.

Coconut is known as the fruit of the gods. In southern India, the coconut tree is considered sacred, because one believes that prayers offered under a coconut tree are always answered. The fruit is needed for rituals pertaining to every festival. On the morning of a festival, prayers are customarily offered before feasting begins. A coconut has to be placed in the place of worship before prayers commence. Every religious ceremony must start with a prayer to the elephant-headed god Ganesha, and his favourite food is placed in front of his statue as a holy offering. Once Ganesha has blessed the food, it is then distributed to everyone in the household.

Rice, ghee (clarified butter), honey, milk, yogurt and sugar are required for every Hindu festival and ceremony. Milk, butter and yogurt were also said to be particular favourites of Lord Krishna. Because of this mythological connotation, these items are considered to be the purest and most sacred of all foods. When a child is first introduced to solid food, it is customary to feed a special dish consisting of rice, ghee, milk, yogurt and sugar as a mark of an auspicious beginning.

As well as feasting, fasting is also an important part of both the Hindu and Muslim religions. The main purpose of observing a fast is the hope of being released from all sins, although emphasis is also placed on the fact that fasting is good for one's system, because it cleanses the body of toxins and gives it a chance to repair itself.

I offer this compilation of recipes to my readers with passion and love, as a kind of thanksgiving for all your letters and e-mails over the years expressing your appreciation of my creations. Nothing can be a greater inspiration than this to a food writer and, as long as you are there to appreciate my work, I will continue to provide you with recipes from one of the finest cuisines in the world!

Mridula Baljekar

Mridula Baljekar

Contents

Great Indian Feasts

Eid-Ul-Fitre
51

Festivals of Goa
65

Durga Puja
83

Mridula Baljekar

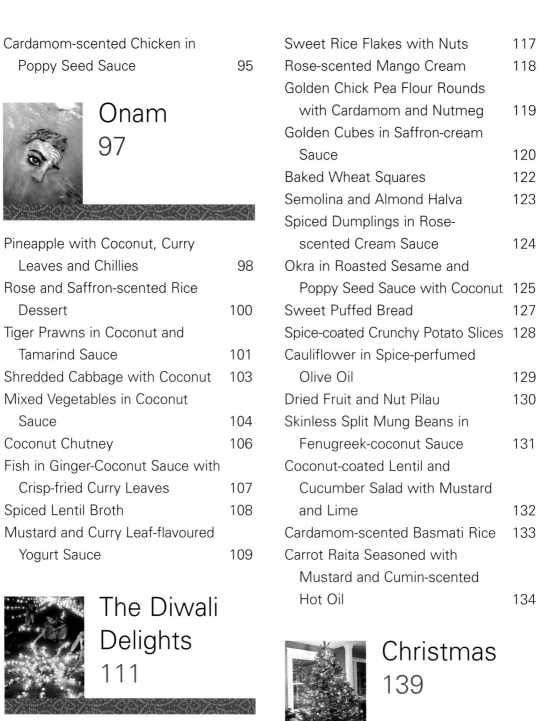

Mridula Baljekar

Lohiri and Baisakhi

The two northern Indian harvest festivals are known as Lohri and Baisakhi. They are both celebrated in the state of Punjab – Lohri in January, Baisakhi in April. The word Punjab literally means the land of five rivers. These large rivers created a very fertile soil, enabling an abundance of crops to grow. Wheat and maize are the major crops here, and Punjab is known as the 'granary of the nation'. Lohri is celebrated in January because the crop that was started in the autumn will by now be showing sure signs of success.

The people of Punjab are fun-loving and energetic by nature. They really go to town during the festival, having music as well as food – their special harvest dance is known as Bhangra. Bhangra music is also very popular in the UK now. Socialising is the order of the day and food is, of course, a part of every social event. This is also the time when they pray for poverty to come to an end.

Dry fruits, sweetmeats made of sesame seeds and savoury snacks similar to Bombay Mix and popcorn are all served. The fields are bursting with mustard greens in the winter, and the Punjabis have delicacies called Sarson ka Sag (a spicy dish of mustard greens) and Makki ki Roti (fine maize flour bread). Punjab is also the home of tandoori food. All kinds of marinated meat cooked in the tandoor are eaten with naan and curries.

Baisahki comes in April, on the first day of the solar calendar. Children are encouraged to give food and money to the poor in the hope of instilling the spirit of giving in them. Baisakhi is celebrated after the harvest. The day starts with a visit to the temple, to offer one tenth of the total crop produced. Village fairs are held, dancing, singing and merrymaking go on until the early hours with food and drink. Chaat, a popular snack, is eaten during this festival along with lassi, the yogurt-based drink, and children enjoy ice cream and candies. Food hampers are also sent to married daughters so that they too can have a share of the successful crop.

In addition, Baisakhi is an important festival for the Sikh community. On this day, their spiritual leader, Guru Govind Singh, laid down the rules of the Sikh religion: (1) not to cut their hair or beard, (2) to always keep a comb with them, (3) always wear an iron bangle on one hand and (4) always carry a small knife (kirpan) so that they can be prepared for battle. For the Sikhs, the Golden Temple in Amritsar is the most sacred. Water from all the holy rivers of India is brought to the tank, which completely surrounds the temple. It is filled with this water. Sikhs believe that a bath with this water will wash away all their sins.

Mridula Baljekar

Spiced mustard greens

Both mustard and corn are grown extensively in the Punjab. Mustard greens are available in Indian stores, but as an alternative you can use a mixture of spring greens and spinach, and add a dash of prepared English mustard for the authentic Punjabi flavour.

Serves 4

450g/1lb fresh mustard
    or spring greens,
    finely chopped
125g/4oz fresh spinach
    leaves, finely chopped
4 tablespoons sunflower
    or vegetable oil
1 large onion, finely chopped
2 teaspoons ginger paste
2 teaspoons garlic paste
1 green chilli, seeded
    and chopped
250g/9oz fresh tomatoes,
    skinned and chopped
1 teaspoon chilli powder
1 teaspoon salt
25g/1oz chilled butter, cut
    into small cubes
Cornmeal Bread and Lassi,
    to serve

In a heavy-based saucepan, bring 300ml/½ pint water to the boil and add the greens and spinach. Cover and cook over a low heat for 25–30 minutes. Cool slightly and purée the leaves along with the cooking liquid.

Heat 3 tablespoons oil in a large saucepan or wok over a medium heat and fry the onion, ginger, garlic and fresh chilli for 7–8 minutes or until the onion is browned.

Add the tomatoes and half the chilli powder and continue to cook for a further 3–4 minutes.

Add the puréed greens and salt. Cook for 10–12 minutes, or until all the moisture evaporates and the greens have a solid appearance. Remove from the heat and transfer to a serving dish.

In a small pan or a ladle, heat the remaining oil over a medium heat and add the remaining chilli powder. Switch off the heat source and let the oil sizzle for 15–20 seconds, then pour the chilli oil over the greens.

Top the greens with the cubes of butter and serve with Cornmeal Bread accompanied by a glass of Lassi, if liked.

Cornmeal bread

Cornmeal (available from Indian grocers) needs to be mixed with fine wholemeal flour or chapatti flour (also available from Indian grocers) for this traditional bread. For an easy alternative, use fine polenta mixed with fine wholemeal strong flour. If you are gluten intolerant, mix the cornmeal with gluten-free flour.

Makes 8

175g/6oz cornmeal
90g/3oz chapatti flour
½ teaspoon salt
1 tablespoon vegetable oil
sunflower or vegetable oil,
   for shallow frying
Spiced Mustard Greens,
   to serve (page 2)

In a large mixing bowl, combine the cornmeal, chapatti flour, salt and vegetable oil together. Add approximately 250–300ml/9–10fl oz warm water to form a moist dough; it is hard to judge the amount of water needed as the absorbency level of flour varies a great deal. Add the water gradually, a little at a time until the dough is formed then transfer it to a pastry board. Knead until soft and pliable.

Cover the dough with a damp cloth and let it rest for 30 minutes. Divide it in half and make 4 equal-sized balls out of each half. Rotate each ball gently between your palms and flatten it to form a round cake.

Preheat a heavy griddle over a medium–high heat.

As this bread is difficult to roll, your skill and patience are required here! You will need to shape each flattened cake into a thin disc by pressing it down then patting and stretching it gently with your fingertips.

To start, generously flour a pastry board then place a cake on the board and press it down with your fingertips and turn it around a little at the same time. Continue doing this (using more flour if necessary) until you have a circle of approximately 10cm/4in diameter. Lift it gently from the board and place on the preheated griddle. Cook for 1 minute and turn it over with a thin spatula or a fish slice. Pour about 1 tablespoon oil all around the edges and let it cook for 1–2 minutes. Turn it over again and add a little more oil. Cook until brown patches appear on both sides. Serve with Spiced Mustard Greens. If you find it difficult to make this bread, and I admit it is not an easy exercise, serve the mustard greens with naan or chapatti – they will taste just as good.

3

Mridula Baljekar

Potato salad with rock salt

During Baisakhi this snack, known as Aloo Chaat, is made at home and is also sold by street vendors. It has a wonderful savoury, tangy-hot flavour and is served cold in small bowls. A combination of black salt and rock salt is used here. Black salt is sold by Indian grocers and it is known to aid digestion, but if you cannot get it use just the rock salt. I like to serve it topped with a tablespoon or more of Bombay Mix for a varied texture which also adds a new dimension to the taste and flavour.

Serves 4–6

750g/1½lb potatoes
2 tablespoons chopped
    fresh coriander leaves
2 tablespoons fresh
    mint leaves
1–3 fresh green chillies,
    seeded and chopped
½ teaspoon chilli
    powder (optional)
½ teaspoon black salt
rock salt to taste
1½ tablespoons
    tamarind juice or 2
tablespoons lime juice
1 small red onion,
    finely chopped
150g/5oz Bombay Mix
    (optional)

Bring a large pan of water to the boil and add the whole, unpeeled potatoes. Cook until tender, drain and allow to cool thoroughly. Peel and dice the potatoes into 1cm/ ½in pieces.

Put the remaining ingredients, except the onion and Bombay mix, in a blender and blend until smooth. Pour this mixture over the potatoes and add the onion. Mix thoroughly.

Put into individual serving dishes and serve sprinkled with the Bombay Mix, if using.

Cumin-scented chicken tikka

In India, a variety of chicken tikka recipes are popular, all of which have their own distinctive appearance and taste. This version has the warm and assertive taste of cumin. Both royal cumin and the standard variety are used here. You can get royal cumin, known as Shahi Zeera from Indian grocers. But, if you cannot get it, just use the standard variety. The yogurt used to marinate the chicken needs to be relatively moisture-free. You can strain plain yogurt through a muslin cloth or use Greek yogurt.

Serves 4–6

900g/2lb skinless chicken breast or thigh fillets, cut into 5cm/2in cubes
1 tablespoon lemon juice
1¼ teaspoon salt or to taste
pinch of saffron threads, pounded
1 tablespoon hot milk
175g/6oz Greek yogurt
6 large garlic cloves, crushed to a pulp or 4 level tablespoons garlic purée
5cm/2in piece root ginger, finely grated or 1 tablespoon ginger purée
½ teaspoon ground turmeric
1 teaspoon garam masala
½ teaspoon chilli powder
1 tablespoon royal cumin
1 tablespoon ground cumin
2 teaspoons chick pea flour (besan) or cornflour
1 teaspoon sugar
50ml/2fl oz sunflower oil
50g/2oz butter, melted

Put the chicken in a mixing bowl and thoroughly rub the lemon juice and salt into the pieces with your fingertips. Set aside for 30 minutes. Soak the pounded saffron in the hot milk and set aside for 20 minutes.

Whisk the yogurt and add the remaining ingredients including the saffron milk, but not the melted butter. Mix well and add this marinade to the chicken. Mix thoroughly until the chicken is fully coated. Cover and leave to marinate for 2–3 hours or overnight in the fridge. Bring it to room temperature before cooking.

Preheat the grill to high and line a grill pan (without the grid) with foil. Lightly brush the foil and 5–6 metal skewers with oil. If you are using bamboo skewers, soak them for 30 minutes first, as this prevents them burning during cooking.

Thread the chicken pieces on to the skewers (reserve any remaining marinade) and place them on the prepared grill pan. Cook 7.5cm/3in below the grill for 5 minutes. Meanwhile, mix any leftover marinade with the melted butter and brush the chicken generously with the mixture. Continue to cook for 3–4 minutes or until slightly charred.

Turn the skewers over and baste with the remaining marinade mixture. Cook for 2–3 minutes or until slightly charred. Remove and serve.

Mridula Baljekar

Tandoori bread

Tandoori Bread or Tandoori Roti is one of the basic breads baked in the tandoor. The original recipe is unleavened, and nothing other than plain water is used in the dough. In an ideal world it should be eaten as it comes off the oven. As my approach to recipe-writing is always more towards the practical side, I have amended the recipe so that you can enjoy it hot or cold.

Makes 8

450g/1lb wholemeal
   self-raising flour plus 1–2
   tablespoons extra for
   dusting
½ teaspoon salt
1 teaspoon sugar
1 sachet easy blend yeast
1 tablespoon olive oil
150g/5oz plain yogurt
225ml–300ml/8–10fl oz
   soda water

Put the flour, salt, sugar and yeast into a large mixing bowl and mix well.

Beat the oil and yogurt together and stir into the flour.

Gradually add the soda water and mix until a dough is formed. Do not worry if the dough feels sticky at this stage. When you knead it, the flour will absorb all the excess moisture. Transfer the dough to a pastry board and knead until it is soft and springy and does not stick to the board any more. You can also make the dough in a food processor if you wish. It is important, however, to mix the dry ingredients first. Put the dough in a large plastic food bag and tie up the uppermost part. Place the bag in a warmed bowl and leave the dough to prove in a warm place for 1–1½ hours.

Preheat the oven to 230°C/450°F/Gas Mark 8. Line a baking sheet with greased greaseproof paper or baking parchment.

Divide the dough into 8 equal-sized portions. Rotate each portion between your palms to make a smooth round ball, then flatten it to form a round cake. Dust each cake in a little flour and roll it out to a 10cm/4in circle. Place on the prepared baking sheet and bake on the top shelf of the oven for 9–10 minutes or until puffed and browned in patches.

Great Indian Feasts

Tandoori chicken

One of the most popular Indian dishes, Tandoori Chicken is relatively easy to cook. I don't like using artificial colours, even in small quantities and in this recipe only saffron, turmeric and hot chilli powder are used to colour the chicken. The rich colour produced by these three ingredients provides the perfect background for the charred patches on the surface of the chicken.

Serves 4

4 chicken joints, skinned
juice of ½ lemon
½ teaspoon salt
pinch of saffron
   threads, pounded
1 tablespoon hot milk
25g/1oz raw cashew pieces,
   soaked in hot water for 20
   minutes and drained
90g/3oz Greek yogurt
1 small onion,
   roughly chopped
4 large garlic cloves,
   roughly chopped
2.5cm/1in piece root
   ginger, roughly chopped
2 teaspoons chick
   pea flour (besan)
½–1 teaspoon chilli powder
½ teaspoon ground turmeric
1 teaspoon garam masala
3 tablespoons sunflower oil
50g/2oz butter, melted
1 tablespoon chopped fresh
   coriander leaves, to garnish
lemon wedges, to serve

Score the chicken joints all over with a sharp knife and rub in the lemon juice and salt. Set aside for 15–20 minutes. Soak the pounded saffron in the hot milk and set aside for 20 minutes.

Place the remaining ingredients, including the saffron milk and the drained cashew nuts, but not the butter and coriander leaves, in a blender and process to form a smooth purée. Pour the mixture over the chicken and rub in well. Cover and leave to marinate for at least 6 hours or overnight in the fridge. Bring to room temperature before cooking.

Preheat the grill to high for 4–5 minutes. Remove the grid from the grill pan and line it with foil.

Lift the marinated chicken with a pair of tongs and place on the foil. Reserve any marinade left in the container. Place the grill pan 13cm/5in below the heat source and cook for 12–15 minutes.

Meanwhile, blend the melted butter with the leftover marinade and baste the chicken generously with some of the marinade. Move the grill pan up 2.5cm/1in for 5–6 minutes or until the chicken is charred in patches. Turn the pieces over and return the grill pan to the original position. Next, baste the chicken with the remaining marinade and continue to cook for a further 5–6 minutes or until charred as above. Transfer to a serving dish and garnish with the coriander leaves. Serve with wedges of lemon.

Savoury yogurt drink

This is the recipe for a basic Lassi to which you can add any flavour of your choice. Traditionally, almost twice the quantity of water is added to the yogurt to make a thin drink, but you can also make it like a smoothie by using less water and adding any seasonal fruit with sugar to taste. The savoury version has cumin and fresh mint, both of which are known to aid digestion.

Makes 1.1 litres/ 2 pints

½ teaspoon cumin seeds
½ teaspoon black
  peppercorns
450g/1lb whole
  milk plain yogurt
14–16 fresh mint leaves
2 teaspoons salt
2 teaspoons sugar
700ml/1¼ pints cold water
crushed ice, to serve

Preheat a small, heavy-based pan over a medium heat and dry-roast the cumin and peppercorns until you can smell the aroma (only about a minute). Transfer to another container, cool and crush them finely either using a mortar and pestle or the back of a wooden spoon.

Put the remaining ingredients, except the ice, in a blender and add the crushed spices. Blend until all the ingredients are thoroughly blended together. Serve in tall glasses lined with crushed ice.

VARIATIONS

For a sweet version, omit the salt and add 50g/2oz caster sugar and 1 tablespoon rose water.

If you want to make a smoothie add approximately 90g/3oz fresh fruit of your choice and adjust the quantity of sugar as fresh fruits will add their own natural sugar.

Mridula Baljekar

Lamb in mint and fenugreek sauce

Known as Methi Gosht, this is a typical Punjabi dish which is enjoyed with rotis (bread) during festivities. Traditionally, fresh fenugreek leaves are used but, as dried leaves are more easily available, I have used them instead.

Serves 4

1 tablespoon unsalted butter
2 tablespoons sunflower oil
5cm/2in piece of cinnamon
  stick, halved
4 cloves
4 green cardamom
  pods, bruised
1 large onion, finely chopped
2.5cm/1in piece root ginger,
  finely grated or 2
  teaspoons ginger purée
4 large garlic cloves, crushed
  to a pulp or 2 teaspoons
  garlic purée
2 teaspoons ground cumin
1 teaspoon ground coriander
½ teaspoon ground turmeric
1–2 teaspoons hot chilli
  powder
175g/6oz chopped canned
  tomatoes including the juice
750g/1½lb leg of lamb, cut
  into 2.5cm/1in cubes
50g/2oz whole
  milk plain yogurt
1 teaspoon chick pea flour
  (besan)
425ml/15fl oz warm water
1 teaspoon salt
2 tablespoons dried
  fenugreek leaves, hard
  stalks removed
1 tablespoon fresh mint
  leaves, chopped

Heat the butter and oil together in a large saucepan over a low heat and add the cinnamon, cloves and cardamom. Let them sizzle for 25–30 seconds and add the onion. Increase the heat to medium and fry the onion until soft, but not brown.

Add the ginger and garlic and continue to fry until the onion is brown. Add the cumin, coriander, turmeric and chilli powder and cook for about a minute. Add the tomatoes and cook until the tomato juices have evaporated. Add the lamb, increase the heat slightly and sauté the lamb for 5–6 minutes.

Beat the yogurt and the gram flour together and add to the lamb. Stir to mix well then add the water and salt. Bring it to the boil, reduce the heat to low, cover the pan and cook for about 30 minutes.

Add the fenugreek leaves and continue to simmer, covered, for a further 15–20 minutes or until the lamb is tender and the sauce has thickened enough to coat the pieces of meat. Mix in the mint leaves, remove from the heat and serve.

Tandoori lamb chops

In India, raw papaya is puréed and used as a tenderising agent for most meat dishes. Make sure you buy a papaya which has a green exterior. Peel it and slice off the very firm flesh from around the entire surface – the pink flesh deeper inside does not have enough papin (tenderising quality) to be effective. It is delicious on its own or can be used in a fruit salad. Alternatively, use 50ml/2fl oz red wine in the marinade.

Serves 4

4 lamb chump chops, total weight about 700g/1½ lb
50 g/2 oz papaya, peeled and chopped (optional)
125 g/4 oz whole milk plain yogurt
5 cm /2 in cube of root ginger, roughly chopped
5–6 garlic cloves, roughly chopped
1 teaspoon each of cumin and coriander seeds
2.5 cm/1 in piece of cinnamon stick, broken up
4 cloves
Seeds of 4 cardamom pods
2–4 dried red chillies, chopped
½ teaspoon salt
2 tablespoons oil
Spiced Savoy Cabbage with Chestnuts (page 170) and Oven-roasted Potatoes with Mixed Peppers (page 171), to serve

Remove the rind from the chops and prick both sides with a fork. Place them in a shallow dish in a single layer.

Place the papaya (if used), yogurt, ginger and garlic in a blender and blend until smooth. If using wine, add it to the chops and set aside for an hour or so, then proceed as follows.

Grind the whole spices and the chillies in a coffee or spice mill until fine and mix with the puréed ingredients. Stir in the salt and pour enough marinade over to cover the chops. Using a fork, mix the meat and marinade thoroughly, lifting and turning to make sure that both sides are coated. Cover and refrigerate for 4–6 hours, or overnight. Bring to room temperature before cooking.

Pre-heat the grill to high. Remove the rack from the grill-pan and line with foil. Brush the foil with a little oil and place the chops on it. Grill the chops about 12 cm (5 ins) below the heat source for 5 minutes.

Mix the remaining marinade with the oil. Turn the chops over and grill for a further 5 minutes, then baste generously with the oil/marinade mixture. Continue to grill for 3-4 minutes and then turn again. Brush with the remaining oil/marinade mixture and grill for 3–4 minutes. Remove and serve, accompanied by Spiced Savoy Cabbage with Chestnuts and Oven Roasted Potatoes with Mixed Peppers.

Mridula Baljekar

Pongal

This southern Indian festival marks their New Year, which coincides with the rice harvest in January. It is a major festival in the state of Tamil Nadu and the emphasis is definitely on rice dishes. On this day, the Sun moves from the Tropic of Capricorn to the Tropic of Cancer. Pongal is a kind of thanksgiving to the Sun God and the Rain God for a successful crop. An abundance of rich crop relies heavily on the required amount of rainfall because of the non-perennial nature of the rivers of this state. In days gone by, Pongal was celebrated only by the farmers, but now it is a national festival. It fosters a feeling of togetherness among family and friends.

The Pongal festivities are celebrated over four days, farmers intermingling with their neighbouring families. The first day is known as Bhogi which is dedicated to Indra the God of Rain. The day starts with a morning bath with sesame oil for the entire family after which they have a bonfire to burn old and unusable items which is supposed to ward off the evil.

The second day is known as Thai, which always falls on 14 January, and is celebrated all over India under different names. Women draw patterns on the floor, outlining them with rice flour and filling the inside with coloured flour. This is known as Rangoli or Kolan, which is a skilful art. Brass and earthenware vessels are decorated with fresh leaves of mango, turmeric and ginger saplings. These vessels are then filled with food and left outside in the sunshine when Surya Namaskar (prayers to the Sun God) is offered by chanting mantras in Sanskrit.

The third day is known as Maatu Pongal. It is devoted to cows and bulls which are supposed to be the symbols of prosperity as well as being invaluable to the farmers. The animals are bathed lovingly by the rivers and small bells are tied around their necks.

The fourth and the last day is known as Kaanum Pongal when everyone starts to unwind with hobbies like gambling! To start anything new on this day is considered to be inauspicious.

Nature features prominently during this time as one day is totally devoted to feeding birds, squirrels and ants with the newly harvested grains.

Mridula Baljekar

Tangy lentils with mustard and curry leaves

This is a superb lentil dish, known as Sambar, which can be served with plain boiled basmati rice or with its traditional partner, steamed rice dumplings (idlis). You can use any vegetable combination of your choice. Diced aubergine on its own makes an excellent choice.

Serves 4

225g/8oz yellow split lentils
   (toor or tuvar dhal)
½ teaspoon ground turmeric
1 carrot, diced into
   bite-size pieces
125g/4oz green beans,
   fresh or frozen, cut into
   2.5cm/1in pieces
1½ teaspoons salt
1 tablespoon coriander seeds
1 teaspoon cumin seeds
1–4 dried red chillies,
   broken up
½ teaspoon black
   peppercorns
½ teaspoon black
   mustard seeds
2 tablespoons tamarind
   juice or ½ teaspoon
   tamarind concentrate
2 tablespoons finely
   chopped fresh coriander
   leaves and stalks

Put the lentils in a saucepan and add the turmeric and 1.1 litres/2 pints water. Bring it to the boil, then reduce the heat to medium and cook for 3–4 minutes or until all the foam subsides. Reduce the heat to low, cover the pan and cook for 20 minutes.

Add the vegetables and salt, cover and continue to cook for a further 10–15 minutes or until the vegetables are tender.

Meanwhile, preheat a small cast iron or other heavy pan or skillet over a medium heat. Add all the whole spices and reduce the heat to low. Stir and roast them until they begin to release their aroma (30 seconds–1 minute). Remove them from the pan, cool and grind until fine in a coffee or spice mill. Add the spice mix to the lentils followed by the tamarind. If you are using tamarind concentrate, stir until it is dissolved.

Add the coriander leaves, remove from the heat and serve.

Spiced potato-filled rice pancakes

These crispy pancakes filled with spiced potatoes (Masala Dosai) are served with a chutney. The pancakes are traditionally made by grinding a mixture of rice and lentils together. The mixture has to be left to ferment first and fermentation can take any time between 6 and 12 hours depending on the temperature. As it is time consuming, I have devised an instant version which is also quite delicious.

Makes 8

FOR THE FILLING
1 tablespoon desiccated
   coconut
1–2 dried red chillies,
   broken up
1 teaspoon salt
2 teaspoons lemon juice
4 tablespoons sunflower
   or soya oil
½ teaspoon black
   mustard seeds
1 large onion, finely sliced
1–2 green chillies, finely
   chopped (seeded if wished)
½ teaspoon ground turmeric
1 teaspoon ground coriander
1 teaspoon ground
   cumin 550g/1¼lb new
   potatoes, boiled and cut
   into bite-size pieces
2 tablespoons chopped fresh
   coriander leaves
coconut chutney, to serve
   (page 106)

FOR THE PANCAKES
125g/4oz semolina
125g/4oz ground rice
90g/3oz plain flour
½ teaspoon salt or to taste
150g/5oz low-fat natural
   yogurt
oil, for frying

FOR THE FILLING
Grind the coconut and chillies in a coffee or spice mill. Transfer the mixture to a small bowl and add the salt, lemon juice and 50ml/2fl oz water. Mix and set aside.

Next, heat the oil in a non-stick saucepan over a low heat. When hot, add the mustard seeds. As soon as they start crackling, add the onion and green chilli and increase the heat to medium. Fry, stirring regularly, until the onions are a light golden colour (8–9 minutes). Stir in the turmeric, coriander and cumin. Cook for 1 minute.

Add the potatoes and the coconut mixture. Stir until the potatoes are heated through and the liquid is completely absorbed by them. Stir in the coriander leaves and keep the filling hot while you make the pancakes.

FOR THE PANCAKES
In a large mixing bowl mix the semolina, ground rice, flour and salt together.

Next, blend the yogurt with 450ml/16fl oz water and gradually add to the semolina mixture, beating well with a wire whisk. Alternatively, put everything in a blender and blend until smooth.

TO COOK AND FILL THE DOSAS
Place a large, heavy non-stick griddle, at least 23cm/9in in diameter over a medium heat and brush the surface generously with oil. Wait until the surface of the pan is really hot.

Pour approximately 125ml/4fl oz of the batter into a measuring jug and spread it quickly and evenly on the pan. Allow the mixture to set and cook for 2 minutes.

Sprinkle 1 tablespoon water around the edges, wait for 15–20 seconds, and turn the dosa over with a thin spatula or a fish slice. Cook for a further 2–3 minutes or until brown patches appear. Fill with the spiced potatoes and roll it up. Serve with Coconut Chutney.

COOK'S TIPS
Make the filling and the chutney ahead of time and refrigerate. Reheat the filling gently in a non-stick pan or in the microwave. Keep the filled dosas hot while you make the pancakes. Put them in a single layer in an ovenproof dish, cover with foil and place in a moderate oven.

Tamarind rice with cashew nuts and coconut

This is a superb combination of rice, lentils and vegetables with a typical southern Indian spice mix and is known as Bisi Bele Huliaana. The lentils used here are known as tuvar dhal which you can buy in Indian stores. Alternatively, use yellow split peas. It is a meal in itself for vegetarians accompanied by a raita. It also tastes superb with any dry spiced meat, poultry or fish. It is traditionally served with melted ghee or butter poured over the rice.

Serves 4–6

225g/8oz pigeon peas (tuvar dhal)
½ teaspoon ground turmeric
salt, to taste
225g/8oz basmati rice, washed, soaked for 20 minutes and drained
4 cloves
2.5cm/1in piece of cinnamon stick, halved
1 teaspoon black peppercorns
125g/4oz green beans, cut into 2.5cm/1in lengths
90g/3oz carrots, cut into small dice
1 tablespoon coriander seeds
2–6 dried red chillies
2 teaspoons split chick peas (channa dhal)
½ teaspoon fenugreek seeds
25g/1oz desiccated coconut
1 teaspoon tamarind concentrate or 2 tablespoons lemon juice
3 tablespoons sunflower oil
1 teaspoon black mustard seeds
20 curry leaves
50g/2oz raw cashew nuts, chopped
melted unsalted butter or ghee, to serve (optional)

Wash the lentils in several changes of water and put into a saucepan with 500ml/18fl oz water and the turmeric and place over a high heat. Bring to the boil, reduce the heat to medium-low and cook, stirring occasionally, for 20–25 minutes until the lentils are soft but not mushy. Add a little more water, if necessary, during cooking. Add salt to taste and mix well and keep hot.

In a large pan bring plenty of salted water to the boil. Add the cinnamon and cloves and the drained rice. Bring back to the boil and cook over a medium heat for 6–8 minutes. Drain the cooked rice and keep hot.

Boil the green beans and carrots in salted water for 5 minutes and drain then refresh in cold water.

Preheat a small heavy-based frying pan or a saucepan over a medium heat and add the coriander seeds, chillies and split chick peas. If the chillies are the long, slim variety, cut them into 2–3 pieces with a pair of scissors. Stir the spices continuously for about a minute when they will release their aroma. Reduce the heat slightly and add the fenugreek seeds and the coconut and continue to roast them until the coconut is lightly browned. Transfer them to a plate to cool. Grind in a coffee grinder. The oil in the coconut will tend to stop the blades from moving; simply scrape it off with a spoon and continue to grind until the mixture is smooth.

Put the cooked lentils, rice and vegetables in a large

shallow pan. If using tamarind concentrate, dilute it with two tablespoons boiling water. Alternatively, microwave with cold water for 30 seconds. Pour the tamarind juice or lemon juice over the rice and mix with a metal spoon or a fork. Next, add the roasted ground spices and gently mix with a fork until thoroughly blended.

In a small pan or a wok, heat the oil over a medium heat and add the mustard seeds. As soon as they start popping, add the curry leaves followed by the cashew nuts. Reduce the heat to low and fry until the cashews are brown. Pour this mixture over the rice and mix well, again only with a metal spoon or fork. Wooden ones will squash the delicate grains of basmati rice.

Served topped with melted butter or ghee, if using.

Steamed semolina cakes

Steamed cakes (idlis) served with spiced lentils (sambar) are Tamil Nadu's (southern India) signature dish. There are two types of cake: one is made with rice and lentils, which are soaked and ground and left to ferment before steaming; while the other, like my recipe, is made with semolina. I have used soda water to speed up the process, and to make the idlis deliciously soft and spongy. Traditionally, Indian housewives use steel idli moulds to steam the cakes in a pressure cooker, but an egg poacher and steamer will do the job equally well. You could use several microwave egg poachers to cook the idlis in a steamer or a standard egg poacher for which a steamer is not required.

Serves 4–5

275g/10oz semolina
1 teaspoon baking powder
½ teaspoon bicarbonate
  of soda
½ teaspoon crushed
  dried chillies
15g/½oz cashew nuts,
  chopped
1 tablespoon finely chopped
  fresh coriander leaves
½ teaspoon salt
225g/8oz bio natural yogurt
425ml/15fl oz soda water
oil, for greasing

In a mixing bowl, combine all the dry ingredients together. Beat the yogurt until smooth then stir into the semolina mixture. Gradually add the soda water and mix until you have a thick paste which should be the consistency of a cake mix, but slightly moister. If the mixture has any lumps, beat it with a wire whisk. Cover the bowl and set aside for 30 minutes (take advantage of this gap to make the lentil dish).

Lightly brush plastic egg poachers with oil or use non-stick egg poachers. Place 1 tablespoon of the idli mix into each poacher and steam them for 10 minutes.

COOK'S TIPS
You can serve the idlis without the sambar as a snack. A chutney, such as Almond Chutney (page 34) or Coconut Chutney (page 106), is an excellent accompaniment.

Lentil fritters with chilli, ginger and curry leaves

These are eaten during Pongal as a snack with tea or coffee. They are also ideal for drinks parties. Serve them topped with bought mango chutney or Coconut Chutney (page 106). The combination of lentils used here are skinless split mung beans (mung dhal) and yellow split lentils (channa dhal) which are traditional. You can use other combinations such as red split lentils and yellow split peas.

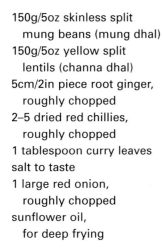

Makes 14

150g/5oz skinless split
   mung beans (mung dhal)
150g/5oz yellow split
   lentils (channa dhal)
5cm/2in piece root ginger,
   roughly chopped
2–5 dried red chillies,
   roughly chopped
1 tablespoon curry leaves
salt to taste
1 large red onion,
   roughly chopped
sunflower oil,
   for deep frying

Mix both types of lentils together and wash them in several changes of water. Soak them in plenty of cold water for at least two hours. Leave to drain in a colander.

Place the drained lentils and the remaining ingredients, except the onion and oil, in a food processor and blend for about 30 seconds. Use the pulse action to blend the mixture to a semi-smooth consistency.

Add the onion and use the pulse button again to chop it finely. The finished mixture should be slightly coarse. Shape the mixture into 14 rounds approximately 2.5cm/1in in diameter.

Heat the oil, in a wok or other suitable pan for deep frying, over a medium heat. Fry the fritters in a single layer in 2–3 batches for 5–6 minutes turning them over halfway through. They should be brown and crisp on the surface and moist in the centre. Drain on kitchen paper.

Fragrant basmati rice with mung beans

This delicious and easy-to-cook dish is known as Ven Pongal. It is made to celebrate New Year and the harvest festival as they coincide in January. The mung beans used are the skinless variety which you can buy in Indian stores. They cook very quickly and really complement the delicate grains of basmati rice. Traditionally ghee is used which gives the dish its distinctive taste. You could use unsalted butter, but take care not to overheat it. If you want to avoid saturated fat, you could use 2–3 tablespoons of sunflower oil as an alternative.

Serves 4–6

225g/8oz basmati rice
150g/5oz skinless mung
   beans (mung dhal)
50g/2oz ghee or
   unsalted butter
1 teaspoon cumin seeds
1 teaspoon black
   peppercorns
2.5cm/1in piece root
   ginger, grated or minced
15–20 curry leaves
1½ teaspoons salt
50g/2oz raw cashews,
   chopped
2 tablespoons chopped
   fresh coriander leaves

Wash the rice and the mung beans in several changes of water and soak them, separately, for approximately 20 minutes. Drain thoroughly.

Reserve 1 tablespoon of the ghee or butter and heat the remainder in a heavy-based saucepan over a low heat. Add the cumin seeds and the black peppercorns. Fry them for 15–20 seconds and add the ginger followed by the curry leaves. Fry them for 25–30 seconds.

Add the rice and the beans, raise the heat slightly and sauté for 2–3 minutes. Add the salt and pour in 700ml/1¼pints hot water. Bring to the boil, reduce the heat to very low and cover the pan tightly. Cook for 10 minutes and switch off the heat source. Leave the pan undisturbed for 10 minutes.

Meanwhile, heat the reserved ghee or butter in a small pan over a low heat and fry the cashews until they are lightly browned. Using a metal spoon, transfer the rice on to a serving plate. Spread the chopped coriander leaves evenly on top followed by the fried cashews along with the ghee or butter in which they were fried. Serve with a vegetable, meat, poultry or fish curry.

Mridula Baljekar

Holi

Holi, the spring festival of colours, is another major Hindu festival. It is associated with the Hindu god Krishna's childhood pranks. He loved to play with coloured water, especially together with pretty women – he had eight wives! Holi is celebrated with light-hearted exuberance and people spray coloured water on each other using a brass syringe known as a pichkari. The pranks played by Lord Krishna on his female companions and those played on him by them in turn are recreated even today, including the songs which were sung.

A few days before Holi, housewives get busy with spring-cleaning and cast aside unwanted possessions for a bonfire which takes place on the first night of Holi. This bonfire signifies the end of the old year and the beginning of the new one.

The flowers of a typical Indian tree, palash (also known as the flame of the forest), are dried and sold especially for Holi. The dried flowers, when soaked in water, add a rich saffron-like colour to it. Tubs of coloured water adorns courtyards and rooftops. This water is also believed to be good for health.

Just before Holi, a special shopping spree takes place and festive dishes like meatballs and meat curries, spiced livers, sweetmeats, lentil fritters and papri (a crispbread made of chick pea flour) are prepared. It is a tradition to invite married daughters with their husbands and his family.

Holi starts on a full moon night and lasts for three days. On the first night, families get together in the evening to launch the formal sprinkling of the coloured water. The eldest member of the family sprinkles colours on the other family members. Then the remaining male members of the family sprinkle coloured water on the rest of the family. Parents present their daughters with a special sari especially for this occasion. Once this ceremony is over, the evening comes to a close with a feast for the family.

On the second day, the community celebrations begin with bonfires lit on crossroads. Snacks are roasted over the fires and alcohol is also permitted during these festivities, and singing and dancing take place in the streets.

On the third and final day, the morning begins with drenching each other in coloured water. Friends and neighbours visit each other with buckets of the water and people travel great distances in cars and buses to do this. This continues well into lunchtime, when a great feast is shared by all and the festival comes to a close. Everyone then heads to the bathroom for a good wash and shampoo.

Mridula Baljekar

Mini chick pea flour crispbread

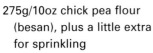

These delicious morsels, known as papri, are delightful on their own or with any kind of topping. For a sublime taste sensation, serve them topped with Potato Salad with Rock Salt (page 4), drizzle any kind of chutney on it and sprinkle with Bombay Mix. When eaten this way, they are known as Papri Chaat. They are ideal at drinks parties and the crispbread will keep well for a week or so in an airtight container. Mustard oil is used in the dough but, if you cannot get it, use 1 teaspoon of English mustard and 2 tablespoons sunflower oil instead. Fenugreek leaves are also used in the dough, but you can substitute these with dried mint or onion seeds.

Serves 6–8

275g/10oz chick pea flour (besan), plus a little extra for sprinkling
1 teaspoon salt
1 teaspoon chilli powder
2 tablespoons mustard oil
1 tablespoon dried fenugreek leaves (kasoori methi)
100ml/3½fl oz water

Combine all the dry ingredients in a mixing bowl and gradually add the water. Mix with a wooden spoon until you have a soft dough.

Transfer it to a pastry board and grease a rolling pin generously. Beat the dough for several minutes, gathering and folding it as you go along. Next shape it into a 15cm/6in square.

Sprinkle the extra chick pea flour on the board and roll out the dough to a larger square which should be fairly thin (slightly thicker than a potato crisp). Use a small biscuit cutter and cut out as many rounds as you can. Gather up the remaining dough and beat again with the greased rolling pin. Roll out to the required size and shape as above and cut out more rounds. Repeat this process until you have used up all the dough.

In a wok or other pan suitable for deep frying, heat the oil over a medium-low heat. Fry as many crispbreads as the pan will hold in a single layer without overcrowding it. Keep the heat on the lower side so that the bread can cook and crisp up at the same time. Frying them over too high a heat will cause them to brown too quickly without being crisp. Drain on kitchen paper.

Masala chicken livers

Chicken liver is inexpensive, extremely nutritious and very quick to cook. Here they are deliciously spiced and sautéed gently to form a light crust leaving the inside beautifully moist and moreish. Serve it with chapattis or soft tortillas or in wholemeal pitta pockets with a salad.

Serves 4

4–5 tablespoons sunflower
  or vegetable oil
1 large onion, halved
  and finely sliced
750g/1½lb chicken livers
1½ tablespoons chick pea
  flour (besan) or plain flour
1 teaspoon salt
1 teaspoon ground cumin
1 teaspoon garam masala
1–2 teaspoons chilli powder
4 large garlic cloves, crushed
  or 2 teaspoons garlic purée
2 fresh ripe tomatoes,
  seeded and chopped
2–3 tablespoons chopped
  fresh coriander leaves

Heat the oil in a large, non-stick sauté pan over a medium heat and fry the onion until well browned (12–15 minutes), stirring regularly.

Meanwhile, clean and wash the liver, drain well and pat dry with kitchen paper. Spread it out on a large plate.

Mix the flour with the salt and spices and sprinkle it over the liver. Sprinkle 1 tablespoon water over if necessary so that the spiced flour clings to the pieces of liver. Mix it well.

When the onions are ready, lift them with a slotted spoon and press the excess oil with a spoon back into the pan. Drain the onions on kitchen paper.

Add the garlic to the oil left in the pan and fry over a low heat for 2–3 minutes. Add half the liver and fry over a medium heat until it changes colour. Remove them with a slotted spoon and set aside. Add the remaining liver (add a little more oil if necessary) and fry for a further 3–4 minutes. Add the first batch of sautéed liver and reduce the heat to low.

Mix 2–3 tablespoons water with any residue of the spiced flour in which you mixed the liver. Add this to the pan and cook for 2–3 minutes.

Stir in the tomatoes and coriander leaves. Remove from the heat and serve.

Mridula Baljekar

Spring chicken in almond and poppy seed sauce

This opulent dish comes from Kashmir in northern India. The appearance of almond blossoms during spring enhances the already unsurpassed natural beauty of Kashmir which is well-known as a veritable heaven on earth. Almonds, walnuts, cherries and peaches are used generously in Kashmiri cooking. For this recipe you can use mature birds if you wish, but I have used spring chicken.

Serves 4

4 poussin breast joints and
    4 leg joints, skinned
125g/4oz whole milk
    plain yogurt
1 teaspoon chick pea flour
    (besan)
2.5cm/1in piece root
    ginger grated or 2
    teaspoons ginger purée
4–5 garlic cloves, crushed, or
    2 teaspoons garlic purée
1 large onion, finely chopped
½–1 teaspoon chilli powder
½ teaspoon ground turmeric
6 green cardamom pods,
    bruised
1 teaspoon salt
1 tablespoon blanched
    and slivered almonds
2 tablespoons white poppy
    seeds
2 tablespoons sunflower
    or vegetable oil
2 teaspoons ground coriander
1½ teaspoons ground cumin
½ teaspoon ground fennel
15g/½oz fresh coriander leaves
    and stalks, finely chopped
1 tablespoon fresh mint
    leaves, chopped
2–3 small green chillies, slit
    lengthways
saffron rice, to serve

Put the poussin joints in a large non-stick sauté pan or frying pan with a lid. Whisk the yogurt with the chick pea flour (whisking prevents the yogurt curdling during cooking), ginger, garlic, onion, chilli powder, turmeric, cardamom pods and salt. Stir over a medium heat until the joints are opaque (4–5 minutes). Cover the pan and reduce the heat to low. Cook for 15 minutes, stirring once or twice. Remove the lid and cook, uncovered, over a medium-high heat until the sauce resembles a very thick batter.

Meanwhile, grind the almonds in a coffee or spice mill until they are broken up into small pieces. Add the poppy seeds and grind until fine.

Add the oil, coriander, cumin and fennel to the cooked poussins and stir over a medium heat for 2–3 minutes. Add the ground almond mixture and reduce the heat to low. Continue to fry until the meat begins to brown (5–6 minutes), stirring regularly. Add 150ml/5fl oz warm water and continue to cook for 2–3 minutes. Add the herbs and chillies. Cook for 1–2 minutes, remove from the heat and serve with saffron rice.

Meatballs in turmeric-tinged yogurt and cream sauce

These delectable meatballs (goshtaba) are made of prime-quality ground meat. The recipe comes from the beautiful valley of Kashmir where housewives take great pride in making the finest goshtaba. The texture of the meat needs to be very fine, so it is best to buy lean lamb and process it to a fine paste in the food processor. Minced or ground spring lamb is ideal for this recipe.

Serves 4

750g/1½lb boned leg of lamb, cut into cubes
50g/2oz unsalted butter or ghee
½ teaspoon ground cardamom
½ teaspoon freshly ground nutmeg
½ teaspoon chilli powder
5cm/2in piece root ginger, finely grated
1 teaspoon dried mint
1½ teaspoons salt
3 tablespoons sunflower or vegetable oil
1 large onion, finely chopped
1 teaspoon ground fennel
1 teaspoon ground coriander
½ teaspoon chilli powder
1 teaspoon garam masala
½ teaspoon ground turmeric
150g/5oz whole milk natural yogurt
250ml/9fl oz double cream
1 tablespoon chick pea flour (besan)
sprigs of fresh coriander, to garnish
Cardamom-scented Basmati Rice, to serve (page 133)

Put the meat in a food processor and process until you have a fine paste. Transfer to a large mixing bowl and add the butter or ghee, cardamom, nutmeg and chilli powder and knead it until it is really smooth.

Add half the quantities of the next 3 ingredients (grated ginger, mint and salt). Knead again to make sure that they have all blended well. Divide the mixture into 2 equal portions and make 10 balls out of each. Rotate them quickly between your palms to make them smooth.

In a heavy saucepan, heat the oil over a medium heat and fry the onions and the remaining ginger until the onions are soft and translucent (6–7 minutes). Add the spices and cook for 1 minute. Reduce the heat to low.

Beat the yogurt and the cream together until smooth and add to the spices. Blend the chick pea flour with a little water (as you would blend cornflour), and add 75ml/3fl oz water. Beat until smooth and add to the spiced yogurt and cream mixture.

When the mixture begins to bubble, add the remaining salt and the meatballs, preferably in a single layer. Cover the pan and cook for 15 minutes until the meatballs are firm. Stir gently, re-cover and cook for a further 15 minutes. Remove the lid for the last 5 minutes, if necessary, to reduce the sauce. Stir in the remaining mint and remove from the heat. Serve garnished with the sprigs of fresh coriander accompanied by Cardamom-scented Basmati Rice.

Mridula Baljekar

Fragrant lamb chops

This is a Muslim-influenced dish known as Rezala and it originated in the kitchens of one of the Mogul rulers who lived near Calcutta before moving on. Traditionally, it is made with mutton rib chops which you can buy in Indian shops with their own in-house butchery. I prefer to cook Rezala with lamb rib chops. If you want to use boneless meat, use lamb neck fillets and cut them into chunky pieces. Rezala is not necessarily a traditional dish during the festival of Holi but, a few years ago when I was in Calcutta during this time, a Bengali family cooked this enticing dish for me.

Serves 2–3

1 large onion, chopped
5cm/2in piece root ginger, roughly chopped
4–5 cloves garlic, chopped
4 cloves
4 green cardamom pods
5cm/2in piece cinnamon stick, halved
½ teaspoon black peppercorns
750g/1½lb lamb rib chops
4 tablespoons sunflower or vegetable oil
1 large onion, finely chopped
175g/6oz natural yogurt
2 teaspoons chick pea flour
50g/2oz butter
150ml/5fl oz single cream
1 teaspoon salt or to taste
½ teaspoon ground fennel
½ teaspoon dried ginger powder
3–6 dried red chillies, soaked in warm water for 10–15 minutes
½ teaspoon grated nutmeg
½ teaspoon sugar
1 tablespoon lime juice
a pinch of saffron threads, pounded and steeped in 1 tablespoon hot water for 10–15 minutes
1 tablespoon rose water

Purée the onion, ginger and garlic in a blender. Add a little water if needed. Put the purée in a bowl and add the cloves, cardamom, cinnamon and peppercorns. Mix well.

Put the lamb chops in a large mixing bowl and add the above marinade. Mix thoroughly, cover the bowl with clingfilm and leave to marinate for 3–4 hours or overnight in the fridge. Bring to room temperature before cooking.

Heat half the oil over a medium–high heat and fry the onions until they are browned. Remove with a slotted spoon, squeezing out as much excess oil as possible, by pressing them to the side of the pan with the spoon.

In the remaining oil, fry the marinated lamb chops for 4–5 minutes, stirring frequently. Reduce the heat to low, cover and cook for 5–7 minutes.

Meanwhile, beat the yogurt with the flour and put it in a small saucepan along with the butter and cream. Place over a low heat and cook for 5–6 minutes, stirring constantly, then add the mixture to the lamb chops with the salt. Add the fennel and ginger powder and cover the pan. Cook until the chops are tender, the length of time will depend on how you like the chops. In Indian cooking meat is never left pink in the middle and the chops would be cooked 30–40 minutes. If you like them pink in the middle then cook them for no longer than 10–12 minutes.

Drain the chillies and add to the chops along with the nutmeg and sugar. Cook for 1–2 minutes and add the lime juice, saffron and rose water. Stir and mix well, remove from the heat and serve with naan or basmati rice.

Almond chutney

In Indian cooking, chutneys are made by grinding all the ingredients to a smooth purée or a pulp. Almonds are very popular in northern India, though quite expensive. Beautiful almond blossoms appear in the orchards in Kashmir, signalling the onset of spring.

Serves 4–6

50g/2oz blanched almonds
1–2 green chillies, roughly chopped (seeded if liked)
1 small clove garlic
2.5cm/1in piece root ginger, roughly chopped
15g/½oz fresh coriander leaves and stalks, roughly chopped
10–12 fresh mint leaves
½ teaspoon salt
1 teaspoon sugar
1 tablespoon lemon juice

Soak the almonds in 175ml/6fl oz boiling water for 15 minutes. Reserve the soaking water.

Put the almonds and their soaking water, along with the remaining ingredients, in a blender and blend until smooth. Transfer to a serving bowl and chill for an hour or so before serving. This is good served with any fried or grilled food.

Spice-crusted fried peanuts

Buy really good-quality, large peanuts to make this divine nibble. A spiced chick pea flour mixture adorns the peanuts in a way that is totally impossible to resist!

Serves 6–8

450g/1lb large, raw peanuts
  skin on
3 tablespoons chick pea flour
  (besan), sieved
1–3 teaspoons hot chilli
  powder
½ teaspoon ground turmeric
1 teaspoon cumin seeds,
  lightly crushed with a
  rolling pin
1 teaspoon onion seeds
½ teaspoon aniseed
1 teaspoon salt or to taste
5 tablespoons water
sunflower oil, for deep frying

Put the peanuts in a mixing bowl. Mix the chick pea flour with all the spices and salt. Add the water and mix until you have a thick paste. Pour this over the peanuts and mix well until the peanuts are thoroughly coated.

In a wok or other pan suitable for deep frying, heat the oil over a medium-high heat. Fry the peanuts in batches for about 2 minutes. Drain on kitchen paper. Cool and store in an airtight jar for up to 2–3 weeks.

Mridula Baljekar

The Easter Table

The origins of the Easter festival date back to Pagan Times. The Anglo-Saxon goddess of dawn was known as Eastre and legend has it that she gave her own name to this spring festival, the dawn of new life, which became known as Easter.

When thinking of Easter, hot cross buns and chocolate eggs instantly come to mind. For something different, I recently tried toasted hot cross buns with rose petal spread, available from Indian grocers. They are wicked!

Festival food is symbolic the world over. For instance, butter and milk-based items are prepared during Hindu festivals, as they were supposed to be the favourites of Lord Krishna. The cross on the hot cross bun at Easter represents the cross on which Christ died, though some believe that it wards off evil spirits.

Eggs, real or chocolate, represent new life. The tradition of eggs also exists because eggs were given to children at the end of Lent, to remind them that 40 days of fasting were over. The fasting period resulted in an abundance of eggs at the end of Lent. Thus, the practice of decorating hard-boiled eggs to give as gifts was born. The tradition of brightly coloured Easter eggs is also associated with the bright rays of the spring sun.

Lamb is served at Easter as a reminder of Jesus. He was considered to be the Good Shepherd, watching over his followers, just as shepherds watch over their flock. In addition, lambs are a symbol of new life, as they are associated with the spring, and also with the ancient Israelite tradition of using lambs' blood to protect their firstborn children.

Recipes for unleavened Indian bread are particularly apt at Easter, as they are symbolic of sacrifices made by Jesus at this time.

In this section, you will find recipes for unusual and exquisite unleavened bread, and other delights to spice up your Easter such as Spring Lamb Roast, in keeping with the traditional Easter Sunday lunch. Spring lamb is also representative of Christ's innocence. Hard-boiled Eggs and Potatoes with Chilli-turmeric Crust will undoubtedly be a novel way of serving eggs at Easter. They are easy to make and will be a talking-point at your Easter celebrations!

Mridula Baljekar

Spiced spring lamb roast

Marinated leg of lamb cooked in a clay oven (tandoor) is a traditional northern Indian dish. The meat is usually marinated in a mixture including unripe papaya purée which contains papain, an enzyme which is an excellent tenderising agent. I have used red wine here as an easily available alternative.

Serves 4–6

1.8kg/4lb leg spring lamb, any membrane and excess fat removed
175ml/6fl oz red wine
1 tablespoon ginger purée
1 tablespoon garlic purée
1 teaspoon chilli powder
3 tablespoons sunflower or vegetable oil
1 teaspoon salt
½ teaspoon freshly milled black pepper
½ teaspoon ground cinnamon
½ teaspoon ground cloves
½ teaspoon ground cardamom
1 sprig of fresh rosemary, pounded
25g/1oz raw cashew pieces
1 tablespoon white poppy seeds
1 tablespoon seedless raisins
2–3 tablespoons milk
pinch of saffron threads, pounded and steeped in 3 tablespoons hot milk
3 tablespoons melted butter
Pilau Rice with Toasted Pine Nuts (page 174) or Mint and Onion Flavoured Flat Bread (page 47), to serve

With a sharp knife, make 4–5 2.5cm/1in incisions on the lamb. Place in a large, shallow dish. Mix the wine, ginger, garlic and chilli powder together. Rub this mixture all over the lamb, paying attention to the incisions. Pour over any remaining marinade and set aside for 30–35 minutes.

Next mix the oil, salt, pepper, cinnamon, cloves, cardamom and rosemary together. Rub this mixture all over the leg of lamb, again, not forgetting the slits. Cover and refrigerate for 24–36 hours. Bring it to room temperature before cooking (1 hour approximately).

Preheat the oven to 220°C/425°F/Gas Mark 7 (adjust the temperature for fan assisted oven according to manufacturer's guidelines). Grind the cashew nuts and the poppy seeds in a coffee or spice mill. The cashews do not have to be fine. Place in a bowl and add the raisins; moisten the ingredients with 2–3 tablespoons milk to make a thick paste. Push this mixture into the slits on the leg of lamb and place it in a warmed roasting tin and pour over some of the marinade in the dish. Cook in the centre of the oven for 20 minutes basting, once or twice. Reduce the temperature to 190°C/375°F/Gas Mark 5 and pour the remaining marinade over the meat. Continue to cook for 30–35 minutes.

Drizzle half the saffron milk over the meat and cook for 10 minutes. Carefully turn the meat and drizzle over the remaining saffron milk. Continue to cook for 25–30 minutes then pour over the melted butter. Cook for 10–15 minutes, remove from the oven, rest for 20–25 minutes and cut into chunks. Serve with Pilau Rice with Toasted Pine Nuts or Mint and Onion Flavoured Flat Bread.

Cheese and potato rissoles with chopped eggs

In east and north-east Indian cooking one still comes across strong British influences. This is one of those recipes which were popularised during the British Raj. Paneer, the traditional unripened Indian cheese would be the natural choice in India, but halloumi cheese also works very well. Do remember to reduce the amount of salt if you use halloumi as it is quite salty.

Makes 12

6 hard-boiled eggs
250g/9oz diced potatoes, boiled and mashed
125g/4oz paneer cheese, grated
3 tablespoons sunflower or light olive oil
1 medium onion, finely chopped
2.5cm/1in piece root ginger, grated
1–3 green chillies, finely chopped (seeded if liked)
½ teaspoon ground turmeric
½ teaspoon fennel seeds, crushed with a rolling pin or mortar and pestle
2 tablespoons finely chopped coriander leaves
1 tablespoon snipped fresh chives
1 teaspoon salt or to taste
2 tablespoons plain flour
1 large egg, beaten
90g/3oz fresh soft breadcrumbs
sunflower oil, for deep frying
green salad, to serve

Shell the eggs and halve them. Scoop out the yolks and mash them. Chop the whites finely and mix the egg yolks and whites with the mashed potatoes and grated cheese.

Heat the oil over a medium heat and fry the onion, ginger and chillies until the onion is soft, 5–6 minutes.

Add the turmeric and fennel, stir and cook for about a minute, then add the coriander, chives and salt. Stir once and remove from the heat. Add to the egg mixture. Stir until the ingredients are well incorporated.

Divide the mixture into 12 equal-sized balls and flatten them into round cakes of approximately 1cm/½in thickness. Dust in flour and dip in beaten egg then roll in breadcrumbs.

Preheat the sunflower oil in a large saucepan and fry the patties until they are crisp and golden brown. Drain on kitchen paper and serve with a green salad.

Mridula Baljekar

Hard-boiled eggs and potatoes with a chilli-turmeric crust

This is one of the most popular dishes in east and north-east India. In celebration and special occasion menus, it features regularly along with Deep-fried Puffed Bread (page 84). The eggs and the potatoes are sautéed with a touch of spices until they form a light crust, then simmered in the fragrant sauce.

Serves 6

6 hard-boiled eggs
½ teaspoon chilli powder
½ teaspoon ground turmeric
5 tablespoons sunflower or
   light olive oil
450g/1lb potatoes, cut into
   2.5cm/1in cubes
6 green cardamom pods,
   bruised
4 cloves
1 large onion, finely chopped
1 teaspoon ginger purée or
   1cm/½in piece root ginger,
   finely grated
1–2 green chillies, finely
   chopped (seeded if liked)
1 teaspoon ground coriander
½ teaspoon ground cumin
½ teaspoon ground turmeric
1 teaspoon chilli powder
200g/7oz chopped canned
   tomatoes with the juice
1 teaspoon salt
1–2 tablespoons chopped
   fresh coriander leaves

Shell the eggs and make 3–4 slits lengthwise on each egg leaving a little gap on either end.

Combine the chilli powder and ground turmeric. In a heavy-based saucepan, preferably non–stick, heat half the oil over a low-medium heat and add half the chilli-turmeric mix. Quickly add the eggs and turn them around in the pan until they are covered with a light crust of spices. Remove the eggs with a slotted spoon.

Add the potatoes to the oil left in the pan and increase the heat to medium-high. Sprinkle over the remaining chilli-turmeric mix and sauté the potatoes until they are brown and have formed a crust. Remove with a slotted spoon.

Reduce the heat slightly and add the remaining oil to the pan. Add the cardamom and cloves and let them sizzle for 25–30 seconds then add the onion, ginger and green chillies. Cook until the onion is light brown and add the coriander, cumin, turmeric and chilli powder. Cook for about a minute and add the tomatoes and their juice. Continue to cook, stirring frequently, until the tomatoes are reduced to a thick paste and the oil begins to rise to the surface (7–8 minutes); reduce the heat to low towards the last 2–3 minutes.

Add the potatoes, salt and 225ml/8fl oz warm water. Bring it to the boil, reduce the heat to low and cover the pan tightly. Cook until the potatoes are tender, stirring occasionally.

Baked minced lamb with whole eggs

Combining eggs with meat is a Mughal tradition which has a strong influence in northern Indian cooking. This recipe makes an economical as well as nourishing family meal.

Serves 4

4 tablespoons sunflower or
  vegetable oil
1 large onion, chopped
2.5cm/1in piece root ginger,
  roughly chopped
4 large garlic cloves, roughly
  chopped
50g/2oz whole milk plain
  yogurt
½ teaspoon cumin seeds
5cm/2in piece of cinnamon
  stick
4 green cardamom pods,
  bruised
4 cloves
1 teaspoon ground coriander
½ teaspoon ground cumin
½–1 teaspoon chilli powder
450g/1lb lean minced lamb
1 tablespoon tomato purée
3 tablespoons single cream
1 teaspoon salt or to taste
½ teaspoon garam masala
1 tablespoon chopped fresh
  mint leaves
2 tablespoons chopped fresh
  coriander leaves
6 medium eggs
chilli powder or paprika,
  to sprinkle
Beetroot Flat Bread (page 44)
  or Mint and Onion Flat
  Bread (page 47), to serve

Mridula Baljekar

Heat half the oil over a medium heat and add the onion, ginger and garlic. Fry until the onion begins to brown (6–7 minutes), stirring frequently. Remove the onions with a slotted spoon, combine with the yogurt and blend to form a purée.

Add the remaining oil to the pan and heat over a low heat. Add the cumin, cinnamon, cardamom and cloves. Let them sizzle for 20–30 seconds and take the pan off the heat. Next, add the coriander, cumin and chilli powder. Stir and return the pan to the heat, add the mince and increase the heat to medium-high. Fry the mince until it is lightly browned and completely dry. Pour in 200ml/7fl oz warm water and bring it to the boil. Cover and simmer, for 15 minutes.

Add the tomato purée, cream, salt and the puréed ingredients. Simmer, uncovered, for 5-6 minutes. Stir in the garam masala. Reserve a little of the mint and coriander and stir the remainder into the mince. Remove from the heat. Preheat the oven to 200°C/400°F,/Gas Mark 6.

Transfer the mince to a shallow ovenproof dish. Using the back of a metal spoon, make 6 depressions on the mince. Break an egg into each depression and cover with a piece of greased foil. Bake in the centre of the oven for 20–25 minutes or a little longer if you prefer the yolks hard. Remove from the oven, sprinkle the reserved mint and coriander leaves over the mince and sprinkle chilli or paprika over each egg. Serve with Beetroot Flat Bread or Mint and Onion Flat Bread.

Beetroot flat bread

The range of Indian bread is vast and interesting. They are also a healthy choice as atta or chapatti flour is made by grinding the whole wheat kernel which is full of bran and germ. If you cannot get chapatti flour, use fine wholemeal flour, but you may need to adjust the quantity of water to make the dough. This recipe includes finely grated beetroot which makes it extra healthy. In Indian homes an iron griddle, known as a tawa (available from Indian stores), is used to cook flat breads. A frying pan or griddle can be used but it must have a heavy base.

Makes 12

225g/8oz chapatti flour
225g/8oz plain flour, plus a
    little extra for dusting
1 teaspoon onion seeds
1 teaspoon salt
½ teaspoon freshly milled
    black pepper
50g/2oz butter
2 small raw beetroots
    (approximately 175g/6oz),
    finely grated
175ml/6fl oz lukewarm water
sunflower oil, for brushing

Sieve both types of flour into a large mixing bowl and add the onion seeds, salt and pepper. Mix well then rub in the butter and stir in the grated beetroot. Gradually add the water and mix until you have a soft dough. Transfer to a flat surface and knead until the dough is smooth and pliable. Alternatively, make the dough in a food processor, but mix the dry ingredients first. In either case, once the dough is made, cover it with a damp cloth and allow to rest for 20–30 minutes.

Divide the dough into two equal parts and make six balls out of each. Flatten them by rotating and pressing them between your palms. Keep the rest of the flattened cakes covered while you are rolling one. Dust each cake lightly in the flour and roll it out to an 18cm/7in diameter circle.

Preheat a heavy griddle or frying pan over a medium heat and place the bread on it. Cook for 30 seconds and turn it over and brush the surface with some oil. Turn it over again and brush the other side with oil. Cook until browned on both sides.

COOK'S TIP
If you are not serving the bread immediately, you can keep it hot for about 30 minutes. Line a piece of foil with kitchen paper and wrap up the bread well. Seal completely by folding the edges of the foil.

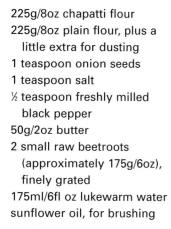

Fragrant basmati rice with carrots and garden peas

For this simple yet attractive and delicious dish, you need pre-cooked rice. You can cook the rice any way you wish, but I prefer to cook it using the absorption method as you do not lose any of the nutrients this way. I have used carrots and peas because I like the bright orange and the dark green against the pure white grains of basmati rice, but you can use any combination of vegetables.

Serves 4–5

275g/10oz basmati rice
2 star anise
4 green cardamom pods, bruised
4 cloves
2 bay leaves
2 tablespoons ghee or unsalted butter
1 large red onion, finely sliced
1 large garlic clove, finely chopped
1 green chilli, finely chopped (seeded if liked)
150g/5oz carrots, cut into julienne strips
125g/4oz frozen garden peas
salt and pepper

Wash the rice in several changes of water until it runs clear. Soak it in cold water for 15–20 minutes and drain thoroughly.

Put the drained rice into a saucepan and add 500ml/18floz water then bring it to the boil. Add the star anise, cardamom pods, cloves and bay leaves. Let it boil steadily for about a minute, then reduce the heat to low. Cover the pan tightly and cook for 8–10 minutes, then switch off the heat source. Let it stand undisturbed for about 10 minutes.

Meanwhile, melt the ghee or butter over a medium heat and fry the onion until soft. Add the garlic and chilli and continue to fry until the onion has browned.

Add the carrots and 2 tablespoons water and stir-fry for 2 minutes. Add the peas and 2 tablespoons water. Continue to stir-fry until the vegetables are al dente. Season with salt and pepper.

Next, fluff up the rice with a fork and, using a metal spoon, gently mix the cooked rice with the vegetables and serve.

Mint and onion flat bread

You have to go through the same process of making the dough for any Indian flat bread. The three stages, ie, mixing, kneading and resting the dough are the crucial points to remember. This bread, with the enticing earthy flavour of chapatti flour (atta) combined with the minty onion, is perfect with Spiced Spring Lamb Roast (page 38) although it is good enough to eat on its own!

Makes 8

450g/1lb chapatti flour plus extra for dusting
1 teaspoon onion seeds (kalonji)
1 teaspoon salt
50g/2oz ghee or unsalted butter
1 tablespoon finely chopped fresh mint leaves
1 medium onion, coarsely grated
125ml/4fl oz lukewarm water
sunflower or light olive oil, for shallow frying

To make the dough by hand put the chapatti flour, onion seeds and salt in a large mixing bowl and stir well. Next, rub in the ghee or butter and stir in the mint and onion. Add the water, a little at a time, as the absorbency level of flour varies from brand to brand. Mix until a rough dough is formed, then transfer to a pastry board and knead for 4–5 minutes, or until it stops sticking to the board and your fingers.

To make the dough in the food processor, put all the ingredients in the processor and knead until the dough feels smooth and soft and it does not stick to the bowl or dough hook. Cover the dough with a damp cloth and set aside for 20–30 minutes.

Divide the dough in half and make four portions out of each half. Rotate each portion between your palms to make a smooth round ball and then flatten it to a cake. Cover them with a damp cloth.

Preheat a tawa, cast-iron griddle or a heavy-based frying pan over a medium heat. Dust each cake lightly in the extra flour and roll it out to an 18cm/7in diameter circle. Place the bread on the griddle and cook for about a minute then turn it over. Spread about 1 tablespoon oil on the entire surface and turn it over again. Cook for 45–50 seconds, or until brown spots appear. Check this by lifting the bread gently.

Spread another tablespoon of oil on the second side and turn it over, then cook as for the first side, until brown spots appear.

Mridula Baljekar

Carrot and cardamom dessert in chocolate cups with mini easter eggs

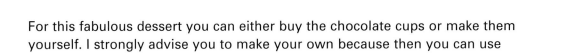

For this fabulous dessert you can either buy the chocolate cups or make them yourself. I strongly advise you to make your own because then you can use chocolate with at least 70% cocoa solids which gives a much more intense flavour.

Serves 6

TO MAKE THE CUPS YOU WILL NEED
greaseproof paper
6 ramekins
2 tablespoons melted butter
175g/6oz dark chocolate

FOR THE FILLING
50g/2oz butter
1 x 2.5cm/1in piece of cinnamon stick, halved
250g/9oz grated carrots
50g/2oz granulated sugar
25g/1oz seedless raisins
200ml/7fl oz orange juice
½ teaspoon freshly grated nutmeg
½ teaspoon ground cardamom
150ml/5fl oz double cream
18 mini Easter eggs, to decorate

Cut out 6 greaseproof paper discs to fit the base of the ramekins and 6 strips to line the sides. The strips should stand at least 2.5cm/1in above the rims. Join the ends of the strips with a little melted butter.

Break up the chocolate and place in a heatproof bowl. Place the bowl over a pan of simmering water and let the chocolate melt completely. Once melted stir thoroughly.

Divide the melted chocolate equally among the ramekins and brush until the base and the sides are coated with an even layer making the top edge ragged. Place them on a tray and refrigerate to set.

To make the filling, melt the butter over a low heat and add the cinnamon. Let it sizzle for 25–30 seconds and then add the carrots. Increase the heat to medium and sauté the carrots for 3–4 minutes.

Add the sugar and raisins and continue to sauté for a minute or two. Add the orange juice and let the carrots cook gently for 10–12 minutes until dry, but still moist. Add the nutmeg and cardamom and mix well. Remove from the heat then set aside to cool.

Remove the cinnamon sticks and divide the filling equally among the chocolate cups. Whip the cream until thick but not stiff. Spoon over the filling and decorate with three mini eggs per cup.

Slow-cooked lamb shanks

This is a top-selling dish in my restaurant and is truly scrumptious. The secret of success here is to keep the cooking pot completely sealed throughout so that no steam can escape. Also, ensure that the heat is low throughout.

Serves 4

4 lamb shanks
175g/6 oz Greek yogurt
One 5cm/2 in piece of
   cinnamon stick, broken up
The inner seeds of
   6 cardamom pods
4 cloves
2 teaspoons cumin seeds
2 dried red chillies, scissor
   snipped
4-5 tablespoons sunflower or
   plain olive oil
1 large onion, finely chopped
5 cm/2 in piece of root
   ginger, finely grated
4-5 large garlic cloves,
   crushed to a pulp
½ teaspoon ground turmeric
½ teaspoon freshly grated
   nutmeg
1 teaspoon salt or to taste
50g/2oz blanched almonds,
   soaked in 150ml/5 fl oz
   boiling water for 20 minutes
10-12 fresh mint leaves,
   finely chopped
Beetroot Flat Bread
   (page 44) or Cardamom-
   scented Basmati Rice
   (page 133), to serve

Remove any excess fat and membrane from the lamb shanks and wipe with a cloth. Prick them all over with a fork. Preheat a small, heavy pan or a griddle over medium heat. When hot, reduce the heat to low and add the cinnamon sticks, cardamom, and cloves. Roast gently until they begin to release their aroma. Transfer to a plate to cool, then grind in a coffee grinder.

Whisk the yogurt until really smooth. Remove half the yogurt and blend it thoroughly with the ground spices. Reserve the remaining yogurt. Place the lamb shanks on a large plate and add the spice-laced yogurt. Rub it in well and cover the plate with food wrap. Leave to marinate in the fridge for 4–5 hours or overnight. Bring it to room temperature before cooking.

Heat the oil in a heavy-based saucepan over medium heat and fry the onions until they are soft and light brown. Stir regularly. Add the ginger and garlic and continue to fry for 1–2 minutes. Add the chilli powder and turmeric, cook for about a minute and add one tablespoon of the reserved whisked yogurt. Cook for 2 minutes and add the nutmeg, salt and the marinated lamb shanks, making sure you add any remaining marinade too. Stir them over a medium heat until the lamb turns opaque. Add the remaining yogurt and 300 ml/10 fl oz lukewarm water. Mix well and bring to a simmer. Cover the pan with double thickness of foil, making sure it does not touch the food, then place the lid on. Seal the edges by pressing the foil into the saucepan rim. Reduce the heat to very low and simmer gently for 40-45 minutes.

Meanwhile, purée the almonds in a blender. Remove the foil from the pan and add the puréed almonds. Stir well and simmer gently for 2-3 minutes. Simmer a little longer if you prefer a thicker consistency. Stir in the chopped mint and serve.

Mridula Baljekar

Eid-Ul-Fitre

The ninth month of the Muslim lunar calendar is the month of Ramadan when they fast during the day, eating only before sunrise and after sunset. This religious practice is observed in order to honour the belief that, during this month, the Prophet Muhammad received his revelation. The day-long fasting ends after sunset when they break it by eating some dates, as their holy book the Quran dictates that they should eat dates, honey, figs, milk and buttermilk. This breaking of the fast is known as Iftar. Then, according to one's means, the entire family shares a lavish feast. A few years ago, when I was in India, I had a fortunate encounter with the Nawab (a member of a royal family) of Hyderabad, who invited me to an Iftar meal. The dinner table, which stretched from one end of the room to the other, was crammed full of exotic food. As we entered the dining room, attentive and uniformed staff offered us water from a silver jug to wash our hands over a silver bowl. I sat next to the Nawab who was very charming and answered all my questions very patiently. The Begum (Nawab's wife) was busy in the courtyard, feeding and giving gifts of clothing to the poor and needy of the city.

At the end of the month-long fasting comes the festival of Eid-Ul-Fitre popularly known as Eid. 'Eid-Ul-Fitre' means 'festival of breaking the fast'. The word 'fitre' is said to be derived from 'fatar' which means 'breaking'. The month-long fast is broken with festivities said to have originated when Prophet Muhammad declared a day of celebrations to follow the 30-day fasting, to promote goodwill among the community.

The day starts with special Eid prayers in the morning. This prayer is known as Do Rakat Namaz. Everyone is required to have a bath before visiting the mosque and the men wear white which symbolises purity. Devout Muslims prepare themselves to bury past discontentment and to forgive. Gifts are given to the poor and needy as thanksgiving to Allah.

Women prepare sumptuous feasts and the celebration table includes such delicacies as pilaus, elaborate biryanis, all kinds of kebabs and speciality breads. Lamb Biryani, Spicy Lamb's Liver, Saffron Bread with Royal Cumin (sheermal) and Sweet Vermicelli Perfumed with Saffron and Rose Water are among the speciality foods you will find in this chapter.

The celebration table includes such delicacies as pilaus, biryanis, all kinds of kebabs and speciality breads.

51

Mridula Baljekar

Lamb biryani

Biryani is a dish in which the rice and meat are cooked together over a very low heat. Its origins are very interesting. The Moguls, Muslims by religion, hit upon the idea of a dry, combination dish which especially suited them on their long journeys of pilgrimage. It travelled well due to the absence of any sauce. Biryani is very similar to the Middle Eastern Pilaff. This is hardly surprising because the Moguls, originally from Persia, came to India via the Middle East and learned some of that region's cooking techniques which they then introduced to India.

Serves 4

90g/3oz ghee or unsalted butter
2 x 5cm/2in cinnamon sticks
8 green cardamom pods, bruised
8 cloves
10–12 black peppercorns
3 bay leaves
1 large onion, finely sliced
1 tablespoon garlic purée
1 tablespoon ginger purée
2 teaspoons ground cumin
1½ teaspoons ground coriander
½ teaspoon ground nutmeg
1–2 green chillies, finely chopped (seeded if wished)
3¼ teaspoon salt
125g/4oz plain yogurt
1kg/2¼lb boned leg of lamb, cut into 5cm/2in cubes
½ teaspoon saffron threads, pounded and soaked in 2 tablespoons hot milk
450g/1lb basmati rice, washed and drained
1 tablespoon rose water
1 tablespoon flaked almonds, toasted

In a heavy-based saucepan (large enough to hold the meat and rice together), melt 50g/2oz of the ghee or butter over a low heat and add the cinnamon, cardamoms, cloves, peppercorn and bay leaves and let them sizzle for 15–20 seconds or until the cardamom pods have puffed up (that's when they release their flavour).

Add the onion and increase the heat to medium. Stir and fry the onion for 4–5 minutes. Add the garlic and ginger, stir and cook for a further 2–3 minutes, then add the spices and chilli. Stir and cook for 1 minute. Add 1¼ teaspoons of salt, then beat the yogurt with a fork (this prevents curdling) and add along with the meat and half the saffron milk. Stir to mix and distribute well and switch off the heat.

Pre-heat the oven to 160°C/325°F/Gas Mark 3.

Put the rice in a pan with plenty of hot water and the remaining salt. Bring to the boil and allow to boil for 1 minute. Drain the rice and pile it on top of the meat. Drizzle the remaining saffron milk on the rice. Melt the remaining butter or ghee and drizzle over the rice.

Soak a large piece of greaseproof paper in cold water and squeeze out the water. Spread this on top of the rice. Soak a clean tea towel and, again, squeeze out the water. Spread it on top of the greaseproof paper and place the lid on the saucepan. Now seal the top of the saucepan with a large piece of kitchen foil so that no steam can escape. Place the pan in the centre of the oven and cook for 55–60 minutes.

Remove the biryani from the oven and allow to stand for 15–20 minutes. This stage is important as the rice will have a chance to absorb any remaining moisture so that you have beautifully dry and fluffy grains. Sprinkle the rose water over and stir the biryani gently with a fork to mix the meat and the rice and serve immediately, garnished with the flaked almonds.

COOK'S TIP
The practice of serving a vegetable curry with biryani is non-existent in India. It is traditionally eaten with a raita but, if you prefer a vegetable curry, choose one from the Diwali or Onam section.

Marinated strips of lamb's liver

Lamb's liver is a traditional item on the Eid table. This recipe is easy and, once marinated, takes only a few minutes to cook under a hot grill. It would generally be served along with all the other dishes, but I think it makes an excellent starter with a little salad to garnish. You need plain yogurt, for the marinade, which has been strained through a muslin cloth to drain off any excess water or simply use Greek yogurt as an easy alternative.

Serves 4–5

750g/1½lb lamb's liver
125g/4oz plain Greek yogurt
1 tablespoon lemon juice
4–5 large garlic cloves,
    roughly chopped
2.5cm/1in piece root ginger,
    roughly chopped
1 teaspoon ground cumin
½ teaspoon garam masala
½–1 teaspoon chilli powder
2 teaspoons chick pea flour
    (besan)
1 teaspoon salt
4 tablespoons sunflower
    or olive oil
6–8 skewers, to serve

Remove membrane and gristle from the liver and wash gently. Dry thoroughly with kitchen paper and cut into 5cm x 5mm/2in x ¼in strips.

Put the remaining ingredients, except the oil, in a blender and make a smooth purée. Put the liver into a non-metallic dish and pour the marinade over. Mix thoroughly, cover the bowl and refrigerate for 4–5 hours or overnight. Bring it to room temperature before cooking.

Preheat the grill to high. Oil the skewers and thread the strips of liver on to them. Grill approximately 7.5cm/3in below the heat source for 5–6 minutes, basting with the oil and turning them over halfway through. Serve immediately.

Mint and coriander-filled lamb patties

These beautifully fragrant kebabs are known as Shami Kabab and are a Muslim speciality. They are made with minced lamb or beef, mixed with channa dhal which is their characteristic feature. Channa dhal is sold by Indian stores and health-food shops, but you can use yellow split peas instead, though the distinctive nutty taste will be missing. The coating with poppy seed is not traditional, but it produces a wonderfully interesting texture.

Makes 16

500g/1lb lean minced lamb
  or beef
125g/4oz channa dhal or
  yellow split peas
2 tablespoons sunflower oil
1 medium onion, roughly
  chopped
5cm/2in piece root ginger,
  roughly chopped
4 large garlic cloves, roughly
  chopped
2 long, slim dried red chillies,
  chopped
2.5cm/1in piece of cinnamon
  stick, broken up
seeds of 6 green cardamom
  pods
4 cloves
½ teaspoon black peppercorn
1 teaspoon cumin seeds
2 teaspoons white poppy
  seeds
1 teaspoon salt
1 tablespoon lemon juice
½ bunch fresh mint leaves or
  1 teaspoon dried mint
15g/½oz coriander leaves
  and stalks

Put the minced meat and the lentils or yellow split peas in a saucepan and add 300ml/½ pint water. Bring to the boil, reduce the heat to medium and cook, uncovered, for 10–12 minutes. Now reduce the heat to low and continue to simmer until the lentils are tender but not mushy (about 10 minutes). The mixture should be completely dry. Increase the heat, if necessary.

While the meat and the lentils are cooking, heat the oil over a medium heat and fry the onion, ginger, garlic and red chillies for 5–6 minutes until browned. Grind the cinnamon, cardamom seeds, cloves, peppercorns, cumin and poppy seeds in a coffee or spice mill until fine.

Put the fried onion mixture and ground spices in a food processor and add the cooked meat and lentils, salt, lemon juice, mint, coriander and one of the eggs. Process until the ingredients are well blended and transfer to a bowl. Cover and refrigerate for an hour or so, although you could leave it overnight. Divide the mixture into 16 equal-sized portions. Have a bowl of cold water ready, moisten your palms and mould each portion of the kebab mix into a miniature cup shape. Mix all the ingredients for the stuffing and fill the hollow with a little of the mixture (it is a good idea to divide the stuffing into 16 equal portions before you start) and cover it completely with the meat, then flatten it slightly to form a 2.5cm/1in-thick cake.

2 large eggs
2 tablespoons plain flour
3–4 tablespoons white
   poppy seeds
sunflower or vegetable oil,
   for shallow frying

FOR THE STUFFING
1 small red onion, very finely
   chopped or minced
1 green chilli, seeded and
   finely chopped
2 tablespoon finely chopped
   fresh coriander leaves
1 tablespoon lemon juice
salad and Apple and Mint
Chutney (page 181), to serve

Beat the second egg, dust each kebab in the flour then
dip in the egg and finally roll it in the poppy seeds. Pour
enough oil in a frying pan to measure about 1cm/½in
depth and heat over a medium-high heat. Fry the kebabs
for 2–3 minutes on each side and drain on kitchen paper.
Serve as a starter with a salad and Apple and Mint
Chutney or as a side dish.

Mridula Baljekar

Pilau rice with mini meatballs

An exotic dish from the Mughal era, this dish is known as Moti Pilau. The word moti means pearl and originally the meatballs were made really tiny, the size of a small pearl. They were also encased in varak, the edible silver leaf, to signify the jewel. If you wish to replicate the indulgent luxury of this bygone time, you can buy varak from Indian stores, but silver dust which is used for decorating cakes works well too. In this recipe I have made the meatballs bigger to save time.

Serves 4–5

14oz/400g basmati rice
450g/1lb lean minced lamb
3–4 shallots, finely chopped
2.5cm/1in piece root ginger, minced or grated
2 large garlic cloves, minced or crushed to a pulp
2 tablespoons finely chopped fresh coriander leaves
1 tablespoon finely chopped fresh mint leaves or ½ teaspoon dried mint
2 green chillies, finely chopped (seeded if wished)
1 teaspoon garam masala
1 tablespoon double cream
175g/6oz whole milk natural yogurt
90g/3oz unsalted butter or ghee
25g/1oz soft white breadcrumbs
2½ teaspoons salt
2 teaspoons chick pea flour (besan)
8 green cardamom pods, bruised
8 cloves
2 x 2.5cm/2in pieces cinnamon stick
2 star anise

Wash the rice and soak it in cold water for 15–20 minutes, then leave to drain in a colander.

Put the minced lamb in a large mixing bowl and add the shallots, ginger, garlic, coriander, mint, green chillies, garam masala and cream. Mix thoroughly and add 1 tablespoon each of the yogurt and the butter or ghee, reserving the rest for later. Now add the breadcrumbs and 1 teaspoon of the salt. Knead the mixture well until smooth, then pinch off small pieces to make the meatballs, about the size of a marble. Rotate each one quickly between your palms to make them smooth.

Whisk the remaining yogurt with the chick pea flour and blend with 300ml/½ pint water. Set aside.

In a non-stick saucepan, melt 1½ tablespoons of the remaining butter or ghee and fry the meatballs in 2–3 batches, until they are browned. Shake the pan from side to side to encourage even browning. Remove them with a slotted spoon and set aside.

Reduce the heat to low and in the same fat fry half the quantity of the whole spices for 1 minute, then add the diluted yogurt, ½ teaspoon of the salt and the chilli powder. Add the meatballs, cover and simmer for 10 minutes. Remove the pan from the heat and transfer the meatballs with a slotted spoon and wrap them up in foil to keep hot. Strain the cooking liquid and add enough water to make it up to 850ml/1½ pints and reserve. In a heavy-based saucepan, melt the rest of the ghee or

½ teaspoon chilli powder
1 large onion, finely sliced
   into half rings
good pinch of saffron
   threads, pounded and
   infused in 1 tablespoon
   hot milk
1 tablespoon rose water
fresh rose petals, washed, to
   garnish (optional)
raita, to serve

butter over a low heat. Add the remaining whole spices and let them sizzle for 25–30 seconds.

Add the onion and fry until lightly browned (7–8 minutes), then add the rice and the remaining 1 teaspoon salt. Fry the rice for 2–3 minutes and add the strained liquid. Bring it to the boil, reduce the heat to low and cover the pan tightly. Cook for 10 minutes then sprinkle the saffron and milk and the rose water over the top. Cover the pan again and let it stand for 10 minutes.

Using a metal spoon, spread half the pilau rice in a serving dish and arrange most of the meatballs on top, reserving a few to garnish. Cover with the remaining rice and place the reserved meatballs on top. You can roll the reserved meatballs in silver dust or wrap them in silver leaf, if you wish. Garnish with the fresh rose petals (if using) and serve with raita.

57

Mridula Baljekar

Liver in tomato and onion sauce

The Muslims in India excel themselves in cooking liver with spices. Here, cubed lamb's liver is sautéed first in chilli-turmeric-flavoured oil then simmered in a rich tomato and onion sauce. A truly tender dish.

Great Indian Feasts

Serves 4

1 large onion, roughly chopped
4 cloves garlic, roughly chopped
2.5cm/1in piece root ginger, roughly chopped
1–2 green chillies, chopped (seeded if wished)
4 tablespoons sunflower or light olive oil
450g/1lb lamb's liver, cut into 5cm/2in cubes
½ –1 teaspoon chilli powder
½ teaspoon ground turmeric
1 teaspoon ground coriander
2 teaspoons ground cumin
125g/4oz chopped canned tomatoes with the juice
1 tablespoon tomato purée
1 teaspoon salt or to tast
75ml/3fl oz single cream
½ teaspoon garam masala
2 tablespoons chopped fresh coriander leaves
boiled basmati rice, to serve

In a blender, purée the onions, garlic, ginger and chilli, adding a little water if necessary. Set aside.

In a non-stick frying pan, heat 1 tablespoon of the oil over a medium-high heat and add the liver and ¼ teaspoon each of the chilli powder and turmeric. Fry until the juices run clear, stirring frequently (5–6 minutes). Remove the pan from the heat and transfer the liver to another dish. Wipe the pan clean with kitchen paper and heat the remaining oil over a medium heat.

When the oil is hot, add the puréed ingredients, cook for 2–3 minutes, then add the remaining chilli powder and turmeric, coriander and cumin. Continue to cook for 4–5 minutes, stirring frequently.

Add the tomatoes and tomato purée and cook for 2–3 minutes. Add 50ml/2fl oz water and continue to cook for a further 2–3 minutes.

Add the sautéed liver, salt and 200ml/7fl oz hot water. Mix well, cover the pan and reduce the heat to low and let it simmer gently for 20 minutes or until the liver is tender.

Add the cream and garam masala, simmer, uncovered, for 4–5 minutes and stir in the coriander leaves. Remove from the heat and serve with boiled basmati rice.

Saffron bread with royal cumin

This luxurious bread is known as Sheermal and is a Muslim speciality which generally graces the festive table during Eid. Traditionally, it is made with equal quantities of milk and ghee. I have reduced the quantity of ghee slightly. The bread is very appealing to the eye with the rich gold saffron strands and the dark brown Royal cumin adorning the surface. It also tastes every bit as good as it looks.

Makes 8

450g/1lb plain flour plus
   extra for dusting
1 teaspoon baking powder
1 teaspoon salt
1½ tablespoons caster sugar
175g/6oz ghee or unsalted
   butter, melted
125ml/4fl oz single cream
200ml/7fl oz warm whole milk
1 teaspoon saffron strands,
   pounded
1 tablespoon Royal cumin
   or caraway seeds
melted butter, for brushing

In a large mixing bowl, mix the flour, baking powder, salt and sugar. Add half the melted ghee or butter and work it in well with your fingertips. Next, work in the cream.

Reserve 4 tablespoons of the milk and gradually add the remainder to the flour. Knead until a soft dough is formed. Alternatively, put all the ingredients (but only half the fat) in a food processor and process until the dough is formed.

If mixing by hand, transfer the dough to a board and add the remaining melted fat. Knead it by gently pressing the dough down and turning it around and over until it is soft, smooth and stops sticking to your fingers and the board.

If you are using a food processor, add the remaining fat and knead until it is soft and smooth and the dough hook and the bowl have no more dough sticking to them. Cover the dough with a damp cloth and set aside for 30 minutes. Preheat the oven to 220°C/425°F/Gas Mark 7.

Bring the reserved milk to the boil and add the saffron strands; stir to mix well. Line a baking sheet with greased greaseproof paper or non-stick baking parchment.

Divide the dough in half and make four balls from each half. Flatten each ball into a round, dust lightly in the extra flour and roll out to a 20cm/8in diameter circle. Carefully lift to the baking sheet and brush generously with saffron milk. Sprinkle with a little Royal cumin or caraway seed and bake on the top shelf of the oven for 7–8 minutes.

Line a piece of foil with kitchen paper and place the cooked bread on one end. Brush lightly with melted butter, and fold the lined foil over it to keep the bread warm while cooking the remainder.

Mridula Baljekar

Sliced lamb in creamy cashew nut sauce

Mughal Emperor Shahjahan, the builder of the greatest monument to love, the Taj Mahal, was renowned for his love of art and good food. This opulent dish was said to have been born during his reign. Lamb curries are very popular during Eid and every family cooks their own favourite for the celebration table. I have used ghee here to replicate the original recipe, but you can use oil instead if you wish.

Serves 4–6

50g/2oz raw cashew nut
  pieces
125ml/4fl oz boiling water
900g/2lb boned leg of lamb
4 large garlic cloves, roughly
  chopped
2.5cm/1in piece root ginger,
  roughly chopped
90g/3oz whole milk plain
  yogurt
50g/2oz ghee or unsalted
  butter
1 large onion, finely sliced
  into half rings
½ teaspoon ground turmeric
1 teaspoon ground cumin
1 teaspoon ground coriander
½ teaspoon ground nutmeg
½ –1 teaspoon chilli powder
225ml/8fl oz warm water
1 teaspoon salt
150ml/5fl oz single cream
½ teaspoon garam masala
1–2 tablespoons rose water
Sheermal (page 61) or Pilau
  Rice with Toasted Pine
  Nuts (page 174), to serve

Soak the cashews in the boiling water for 15–20 minutes. Purée the nuts and their soaking water. Wrap the lamb in a piece of clingfilm and beat with a meat mallet to flatten it to a thickness of about 5mm/¼in. Cut the flattened meat into thin slices, about 5 x 1cm/2in x ½in. Put the garlic, ginger and yogurt in a blender and process until you have a smooth purée.

In a heavy-based saucepan, melt the ghee or butter over a medium heat, then add the onion and fry, stirring frequently, until lightly browned (6–8 minutes). Reduce the heat to low and add the spices. Cook for about a minute and add the meat. Increase the heat to high and stir-fry the meat for 3–4 minutes until it changes colour. Add 2 tablespoons of the blended ingredients and stir-fry for 2–3 minutes. Repeat this process until you have used up all the blended yogurt mixture.

Reduce the heat and continue to cook the meat, stirring frequently, for 4–5 minutes. When the fat floats to the surface, add the warm water and the salt, bring to the boil, cover and reduce the heat to low. Simmer until the meat is really tender (45–50 minutes), stirring occasionally.

Reserve one tablespoon of the cream and add the remainder, along with the cashew nut purée. Simmer gently, uncovered, for 6–7 minutes. Stir in the garam masala and the rose water. Transfer to a serving dish and swirl the reserved cream on top. Serve with Sheermal or Pilau Rice with Toasted Pine Nuts.

Sweet saffron-scented vermicelli

Sweet vermicelli is synonymous with Eid just as a rich fruit cake is with Christmas. This is a quick and easy recipe and the spice-perfumed strands of golden vermicelli are quite divine. Generally, it is served on its own, but I like to serve it with crème fraîche mixed with icing sugar and finely grated orange zest.

Serves 6

125g/4oz plain vermicelli
50g/2oz ghee or unsalted butter
25g/1oz sultanas
25g/1oz raw cashew pieces
4 green cardamom pods, bruised
2.5cm/1in piece of cinnamon stick, halved
½ teaspoon ground cardamom
½ teaspoon ground nutmeg
300ml/10fl oz water
75g/3oz granulated sugar
pinch of saffron threads, pounded and soaked in 2 tablespoons hot milk
25g/1oz flaked almonds, toasted
1 tablespoon rose water
fresh rose petals, washed, to garnish (optional)

Break up the clusters of vermicelli into small portions.

Melt 1 tablespoon of the ghee or butter over a low heat and fry the sultanas until they puff up. Remove them with a slotted spoon. Next brown the cashews in the same fat, remove and set aside.

Add the remaining fat to the pan and add the whole cardamom and cinnamon. When the cardamom pods begin to puff up, add the vermicelli and raise the heat to medium. Fry until it turns a rich golden colour (about 5 minutes), stirring constantly. Remove the pan from the heat and add the sultanas, half the cashews, ground cardamom and nutmeg and stir to mix thoroughly.

Return the pan to the heat and add the water and sugar. Bring to the boil and add the saffron milk. Reduce the heat to low, cover the pan and simmer for 5 minutes. Increase the heat to medium and cook the vermicelli, uncovered, stirring constantly for 2–3 minutes or until the water dries up. Remove from the heat and gently mix in half the flaked almonds.

Transfer to a serving dish and sprinkle the rose water on top then garnish with the reserved cashews and flaked almonds. Serve surrounded by fresh rose petals (if using).

Mridula Baljekar

Festivals of Goa

Goa, on the west coast of India, drips with history and heritage. The Portuguese colonised this area until 1963. They annexed Goa at the height of their imperial power and developed it into a resplendant and impressive region. By the end of the sixteenth century Goa was known as the Pearl of the East, and this grandeur is still evident today.

Here, festivals are a way of life. In this densely populated small state, people belonging to three different religions live in complete harmony and enjoy each other's festivals. The famous Festival of Goa is celebrated before the period of Lent. It is a blend of Portuguese and Latin American influences. Every family, no matter how poor, would save for the special meal on this day. On the Monday after the 5th Sunday of Lent, a procession takes place with all 26 statues of the saints. It is said to be the only one of its kind outside Rome. As this festival falls in the spring, the Hindu festival of splendid colour, Holi, is celebrated to mark the onset of spring. There are several smaller festivals celebrated throughout the year, including Id-e-Milad in November in honour of the Muslim prophet Muhammad. As the year draws to a close, Goa wears a festive look for the Christian festival of Christmas. As well as fun fairs, food plays an important role during this time.

The influence of European culture on Goa's heritage is reflected in its cuisine.

Eating Goan food can be a unique experience. It is a perfect blend of East and West, matching richness with simplicity. Rich ingredients, found locally, have been skilfully utilised with simple cooking methods to create a cuisine which pampers the palate beyond belief.

Goans practically live off their land. Rice is grown in the huge patchwork of paddy fields and fish and other seafood is found along the coast. Generally, meat, fish and seafood and vegetables are cooked in rich coconut milk extracted from fresh coconuts which are grown extensively. They even make their own unique vinegar with fermented coconut toddy.

The Goans cook pork and chicken dishes for festive occasions. The all-time favourite within Goa is Sorpotel, which is served with Sannas, little steamed rice cakes. At Christmas they make trays of sweets and visit their neighbours with sweets, which they enjoy with a glass of Feni, the local liqueur made of the fermented sap of the coconut palm tree. Another famous Christmas speciality is a coconut cake, known as Bibinca. One 20cm/8in round cake needs 12 egg yolks!

65

Mridula Baljekar

Chicken in roasted coconut, poppy seed and peanut sauce

The Portuguese name for this dish is Galinha Xacutti, in which 11 types of roasted spices are used to make an opulent sauce. I love this dish for its accent of roasted spices and the contrast in tastes and texture. When roasting the spices, do keep to the order given, as some spices need less time than others and prolonged roasting will do little to enhance their flavour.

Serves 4

750g/1½lb skinned chicken
  thigh fillets, halved
½ teaspoon salt
4 tablespoons lemon juice
1 teaspoon black mustard
  seeds
4 cloves
5cm/2in piece of cinnamon
  stick, broken
¼ whole nutmeg
1 teaspoon fennel seeds
2 teaspoons coriander seeds
2–6 dried red chillies
½ teaspoon fenugreek seeds
1 tablespoons white poppy
  seeds
90g/3oz desiccated coconut
25g/1oz roasted salted peanuts
4 tablespoons oil
1 large onion, finely chopped
6 large garlic cloves, crushed
  or 1 tablespoon garlic purée
4cm/1½in piece root ginger,
  finely grated
½ teaspoon turmeric
1 teaspoon sugar
3 tablespoons cider vinegar
3–4 green chillies, seeded and
  cut into julienne strips,
  to garnish
plain basmati rice, to serve

Rub the salt and lemon juice into the chicken and set aside for 30 minutes.

Preheat a heavy-based frying pan or a small saucepan over a medium heat and dry roast the mustard seeds, cloves, cinnamon, nutmeg, fennel, coriander and red chillies for about a minute. Then add the fenugreek and poppy seeds. Continue to roast until the poppy seeds are just a shade darker then add the coconut and stir the ingredients around until the coconut is lightly browned. Remove from the pan, cool and add the peanuts. Grind the roasted ingredients, in batches if necessary, in a coffee or spice mill until fine. You will need to stop and scrape off the blades once or twice as the oil in the coconut, poppy seeds and peanuts will stop them from moving freely.

Heat the oil over a medium heat and fry the onion until soft. Add the garlic and ginger and fry for 3–4 minutes, stirring. Add the roasted, ground ingredients and cook for about 1 minute.

Add the chicken and cook for about 5 minutes, stirring until the chicken turns opaque. Stir in the turmeric and sugar. Add 250ml/9fl oz warm water, bring to the boil, reduce the heat to low, cover and simmer until the chicken is tender. Stir occasionally to ensure that the thickened sauce does not stick to the bottom of the pan.

Stir in the vinegar and simmer for 2–3 minutes. Serve garnished with the green chillies accompanied by plain boiled basmati rice.

Pork vindaloo

Goa's signature dish vindaloo is not the palate-scorching dish as it is believed to be. Instead, it is a beautifully prepared dish with an amicable blend of chillies and spices. The traditional meat used for vindaloo is pork, but you can use beef or lamb if you prefer. The name vindaloo is derived from two Portuguese words, 'vin' meaning vinegar and 'alho' meaning garlic. The Portuguese way of spelling it is 'vindalhoo'. When the Portuguese set off on their long voyage to India, they preserved pork in vinegar, garlic and black pepper, to make it last through the journey. Once the recipe reached India, it was Indianised by the local people!

Serves 4

2–6 dried red chillies
25g/1oz root ginger, roughly chopped
25g/1oz garlic cloves, roughly chopped
125ml/4fl oz cider vinegar
1 tablespoon tamarind or lime juice
1 teaspoon cumin seeds
1 teaspoon coriander seeds
6 cloves
5cm/2in piece of cinnamon stick, broken up
8–10 black peppercorns
1 blade mace
seeds of 2 black cardamom pods
½ teaspoon fenugreek seeds
750g/1½lb pork leg steaks, cut into 2.5cm/1in cubes
4 tablespoons oil
2 large onions, finely chopped
1 teaspoon salt
1 teaspoon dark brown sugar
2 teaspoons sunflower or vegetable oil
8–10 curry leaves
plain boiled basmati rice, to serve

Soak the chillies in hot water for 10–15 minutes until softened. Put them into a blender along with the ginger, garlic, vinegar and tamarind or lime juice. Blend until you have a smooth purée.

Grind the cumin, coriander, cloves, cinnamon, black peppercorns, mace, cardamom and fenugreek seeds in a coffee or spice mill until you have a fine powder. Add this to the puréed ingredients and make a paste. Rub about a quarter of the spice paste into the meat and set aside for 30 minutes.

Heat the oil in a heavy-based saucepan over a medium heat and fry the onions until they are lightly browned (8–10 minutes), stirring frequently. Add the reserved spice paste and fry for 5–6 minutes, stirring continuously. Sprinkle in a little water occasionally to prevent the spices from sticking to the bottom of the pan.

Add the marinated pork and sauté for 5–6 minutes. Add the salt and sugar and pour in 250ml/9fl oz warm water. Bring to the boil, reduce the heat to low and simmer until the meat is tender.

In a very small pan or a ladle, heat the oil over a medium heat. When hot, switch off the heat source and add the curry leaves. Let them sizzle for 15–20 seconds and stir the flavoured oil into the vindaloo. Serve with plain boiled basmati rice.

Mridula Baljekar

Spicy roast pork

Goa is well known for its unique cuisine which evolved during the centuries of Portuguese colonisation. This dish is known as Assado De Leitoa, a deliciously spiced roast pork which is marinated overnight.

Serves 4–5

1kg/2¼ lb boneless leg
  of pork
4 tablespoons white wine
  or cider vinegar
1½ teaspoons salt
1½ teaspoons cumin seeds
1 teaspoon black
  peppercorns
1–4 dried red chillies,
  chopped
5cm/2in piece of cinnamon
  stick, broken up
6 cloves
1 teaspoon ground turmeric
1 whole bulb of garlic (12–14
  cloves), crushed to a pulp
  or puréed
5cm/2in piece root ginger,
  finely grated
1 glass dry white wine
4 tablespoons sunflower or
  light olive oil
2 large onions, finely sliced
2–4 green chillies, seeded
  and cut into julienne strips
flat bread, to serve

Remove the trussing and the crackling from the joint. Score it on all sides with a sharp knife. Rub in the vinegar followed by the salt and set aside for 30 minutes.

Place the cumin seeds, peppercorns, red chillies, cinnamon and cloves in a coffee or spice mill and grind until fine. Transfer it to a mixing bowl and add the turmeric, garlic and ginger. Add 3–4 tablespoons water to make a thick paste and rub it well into the pork. Cover and refrigerate overnight. Bring it to room temperature before cooking.

Preheat the oven to 200°C/400°F/Gas Mark 6. Place the marinated pork into a roasting tin and roast just above the centre of the oven for 20 minutes. Reduce the temperature to 190°C/375°F/Gas Mark 5. Spoon half the wine over the joint and cook for 15 minutes. Turn it over and spoon the remaining wine over and cook for 35–40 minutes, basting frequently with the pan juices. Transfer the joint to a lower shelf for the last 10–15 minutes.

Remove the joint from the oven and set aside to cool. Do not wash the roasting tin. When the meat is cool enough to handle, slice it into thick strips.

In a frying pan or sauté pan, heat the oil over a medium heat and fry the onions for 9–10 minutes until light brown, stirring regularly. Add the sliced meat and the chillies. Fry for 6–8 minutes until well browned.

Add 150ml/5fl oz boiling water to the roasting tin and scrape off all the cooking residues. Strain the juice into the meat, cook for 1–2 minutes, remove from the heat and serve with flat bread of your choice.

Great Indian Feasts

Stuffed mackerel with coconut, garlic and chilli

One of greatest delights from the fish and seafood recipes found in Goa, this dish is known as Recheade. Oily fish is best eaten really fresh – choose fish with bright, sparkling eyes.

Serves 4

4 small mackerel, total weight 1.1kg/2½lb, gutted, cleaned, heads, fins and back bones removed
½ teaspoon salt
1 tablespoon lime juice
15g/½oz desiccated coconut
75ml/3fl oz very hot water
4 garlic cloves, chopped
2.5cm/1in piece root ginger, chopped
2 green chillies, chopped (seeded, if liked)
1 dried red chilli, chopped
2 tablespoons tamarind or lime juice
1 teaspoon ground cumin
50g/2oz plain flour
¼ teaspoon salt
¼ teaspoon freshly milled black pepper
sunflower oil, for frying
boiled basmati rice and a lentil side dish, to serve

Put the fish on a large plate, skin side down and gently rub in the salt and lime juice on the upper side. Set aside for 30 minutes.

Soak the coconut in hot water and set aside for 10 minutes then place it in a blender along with the water in which it was soaked. Add the garlic, ginger, fresh and dried chillies, tamarind or lime juice, cumin and salt. Purée the ingredients until smooth and divide into four equal portions. Fill the fish with the stuffing, leaving a 5mm/¼in border. Don't worry if it appears overstuffed, the flour used later will soak up any extra stuffing.

Tie the fish up with cotton or twine in a criss-cross pattern so that the stuffing is held intact.

Pour a little oil into a large non-stick frying pan and heat over a medium heat.

On a large plate, mix the flour, salt and pepper together. Coat each fish generously with the seasoned flour and fry until golden brown on both sides, about 10–12 minutes. Drain on kitchen paper. Serve with boiled basmati rice and a lentil side dish.

Mridula Baljekar

Prawn cake

Prawn cake, or Apa de Camarao, consists of a spicy prawn filling layered between thin omelettes. In Goa, they cover the entire cake with mayonnaise to make it look like an iced cake. I have left it plain here.

Serves 4

FOR THE FILLING
250g/9oz cooked peeled
    prawns
2–3 tablespoons sunflower
    or light olive oil
1 teaspoon fennel seeds,
    crushed
1 medium onion, finely
    chopped
1cm/½in piece root ginger,
    finely grated
2 cloves garlic, crushed or
    minced
1 teaspoon ground coriander
½ teaspoon chilli powder
½ teaspoon salt
1 tablespoon tomato purée
1 tablespoon Greek yogurt

FOR THE OMELETTES
6 medium eggs
1 green chilli, very finely
    chopped or minced
    (seeded if liked)
2 tablespoons very finely
    chopped fresh coriander
    leaves
salt and freshly milled black
    pepper
sunflower or light olive oil,
    for frying
bread, to serve

Using a large knife or a food processor with the pulse action, chop the prawns coarsely.

Heat the oil over a medium heat and add the crushed fennel seeds. Let them sizzle for 15–20 seconds and add the onion. Fry until the onion until it is soft (about 5 minutes) and add the ginger and garlic. Cook for 2–3 minutes and add the ground coriander and chilli powder. Cook for about a minute and add the prawns, salt and tomato purée. Stir and mix well, remove from the heat and stir in the yogurt. Do not cook the prawns over heat as they will start releasing their juices; the filling should be a thick, moist mixture which has no extra liquid. Keep the filling warm by placing a lid on the pan while you make the omelettes.

To make the omelettes, beat the eggs and add the chillies and coriander leaves. Season with salt and pepper.

In a 15cm/6in non-stick frying pan, heat 1–2 teaspoons oil over a medium–low heat. Add two tablespoons of the beaten egg mixture, making sure you take in some of the chilli and coriander leaves, and spread it quickly over the surface of the pan. Allow to set and brown then turn or toss over and brown the other side. Make the remaining omelettes the same way. Pile them on top of one another placing a piece of kitchen paper between each one.

Put an omelette on a dish, spread with a little filling and top with another omelette. Continue layering this way until you have used up all the omelettes. Cut into wedges and serve with bread. This dish is not eaten piping hot, but you could heat it gently in the microwave if you wish.

Great Indian Feasts

Goan pork pies

These lovely little pork pies (empadinha) are made with a rich butter and egg pastry and filled with generously spiced minced pork. They are ideal for buffet parties. The filling can be prepared in advance and once made, the uncooked pies can also be frozen. The pastry is very tolerant and does not mind being kneaded and rolled.

Makes 20

4 tablespoons sunflower oil
1 teaspoon cumin seeds
450g/1lb lean minced pork
1 medium onion, finely chopped
1 tablespoon grated or puréed
   root ginger
1 tablespoon minced or
   puréed garlic
1–2 fresh red chillies, finely
   chopped (seeded if wished)
2 dried red chillies
½ teaspoon black peppercorns
5cm/2in piece of cinnamon
   stick, broken up
6 cloves
seeds of 6 green cardamom
   pods
1 teaspoon cumin seeds
1 tablespoon coriander seeds
1 teaspoon salt
1 teaspoon sugar
2 tablespoons cider vinegar
175g/6oz chopped canned
   tomatoes including the juice
2–3 tablespoons fresh
chopped coriander leaves

FOR THE PASTRY
400g/14oz self–raising flour
1 teaspoon salt
1 tablespoon caster sugar
1 teaspoon caraway seeds
125g/4oz butter, melted
3 medium eggs, beaten
1 egg yolk, beaten
oil, for greasing

Heat 1 tablespoon of the oil over a medium heat and add the cumin seeds followed by the minced pork. Raise the heat slightly and stir–fry the pork until it is completely dry. Remove from the heat.

Heat the remaining oil over a medium heat and add the onion; fry until it is just beginning to brown. Add the ginger, garlic and fresh chillies and continue to fry, stirring frequently, until they are golden brown.

Place the dried red chillies, black peppercorns, cinnamon stick, cloves, cardamom seeds, cumin seeds, and coriander seeds in a spice mill or coffee mill and grind to a fine powder. Add the ground spices to the pan, reduce the heat to low and cook for 1–2 minutes. Add the pork, salt and sugar. Stir–fry for 5–6 minutes and pour in 75ml/3fl oz warm water, the vinegar and tomatoes. Bring to the boil, reduce the heat to low and simmer, covered, for 12–15 minutes. The mixture should be dry, but moist. Cook uncovered, if necessary, to allow for further evaporation.

Stir in the coriander leaves, remove from the heat and allow to cool completely.

To make the pastry, put the flour, salt, sugar and caraway seeds into a large mixing bowl and mix thoroughly. Next, add the melted butter and the whole beaten eggs. Mix the ingredients until a soft dough is formed. Knead for 4–5 minutes until it feels soft. Cover with a damp cloth and set aside for 30 minutes.

Preheat the oven to 200°C/400°F/Gas Mark 6. Brush a 12-section muffin tin with a little oil.

Divide the pastry into 4 portions and roll out each portion into a 25cm/10in diameter circle. Keep the remaining portions covered until required. Using a 9cm/3½in pastry cutter, cut 12 rounds and line the muffin tin. Fill each section with a tablespoon of the minced pork and moisten the edges with water. Cut out 12 lids, 7.5cm/3in in diameter and moisten the underside with water. Place them on top of the filled pies. Press the edges lightly together, brush each pie with egg yolk and make two small slits in each one. Bake in the centre of the oven for 15 minutes or until browned. Remove and cool on a wire rack. Prepare and bake the remaining 8 pies in the same way.

Steamed rice cakes

Mridula Baljekar

These are known as Sanna and are made during festive seasons. Rice is soaked overnight, then ground and allowed to ferment. To aid fermentation, Goans use toddy, a vinegar made from the sap of the coconut palm tree. I have adapted the recipe to use ground rice and easy blend yeast.

Makes 14

90g/3oz desiccated coconut
275g/10oz ground rice
2½ teaspoons easy blend
    yeast
1 teaspoon sugar
1 teaspoon salt
Gin-laced Pork and Pig's Liver
    with Cinnamon and Cloves,
    to serve (page 77)

Grind the coconut in a coffee grinder until fine then soak it in 175ml/6fl oz hot water and leave to cool until it is lukewarm. This is important as the yeast will not activate if the temperature is too high or too low.

In a large bowl, mix together the ground rice, yeast, sugar and salt. Gradually add 300ml/½ pint lukewarm water and mix with a wooden spoon until a thick batter is formed. Stir in the soaked coconut along with any liquid, mix well, cover the bowl and leave in a warm place for about an hour.

To cook in a steamer or pressure cooker, put 1 heaped tablespoon of the prepared batter into 6–8 small well-greased bowls or ramekins (egg poachers are also ideal for this). Place in a steamer and steam for 10–12 minutes. If using a pressure cooker, steam without the weight. Cook the remaining mixture in the same way. Serve with Gin-laced Pork and Pig's Liver with Cinnamon and Cloves.

COOK'S TIP
Keep the first batch of rice cakes warm, while you cook the second, by wrapping them up in two layers of foil.

Mixed meat stew

Like a lot of Goan food, this stew is a perfect example of the harmonious blend of the three predominant religions – Hinduism, Islam and Christianity. Unlike the other parts of India, beef and pork are sold and consumed freely by the Christians while Hindus will not eat beef and Muslims are forbidden to eat pork. The religious harmony that exists in Goa today owes its success to the Jesuit Father Francis Xavier who arrived from Portugal in the 16th century. In Goa, homemade spiced sausages are used along with other cuts of meat in this stew. You can buy any spicy sausages from the wide range available in supermarkets.

Serves 4

175g/6oz trimmed lean
    stewing beef
175g/6oz boned and trimmed
    pork, preferably from the leg
175g/6oz skinned and boned
    chicken thighs
175g/6oz fresh spicy sausage
4 tablespoons sunflower or
    light olive oil
1 large onion, halved and
    finely sliced
4 large garlic cloves garlic,
    crushed
4cm/1½in piece root ginger,
    grated
1 teaspoon ground turmeric
1 chicken stock cube
1 beef stock cube
450ml/16fl oz warm water
6 whole cloves
2 x 5cm/2in pieces of
    cinnamon sticks, halved
175g/6oz potatoes, peeled
    and cut into 2.5cm/1in cubes
1 teaspoon ground cumin
150ml/5fl oz single cream
½ teaspoon salt
½–1 teaspoon freshly milled
    black pepper
boiled basmati rice, to serve

Cut the beef, pork and chicken into 2.5cm/1in cubes. Grill the sausages until well browned. Cool and cut each into 3–4 pieces.

Put the beef in a saucepan and add 125ml/4fl oz water. Gradually bring to the boil over a medium heat. Cover the pan and cook for 15–20 minutes or until the beef is completely dry. Remove from the heat and set aside.

Heat the oil over a medium heat in a heavy-based saucepan and fry the onion until it is soft but not brown.

Add the boiled beef, pork, garlic, ginger and turmeric. Stir and fry for 3–4 minutes. Add the stock cubes blended with the warm water, cloves and cinnamon. Bring to the boil, cover the pan and simmer for 20 minutes. Add the chicken and bring back to the boil. Cover and simmer for 10 minutes.

Add the potatoes, sausages and cumin. Cover and simmer for 20–25 minutes or until the potatoes are tender.

Add the cream, salt and pepper, stir and mix well. Simmer uncovered for 5–6 minutes, then remove from the heat. Serve with plain boiled basmati rice.

Gin-laced pork and pig's liver with cinnamon and cloves

This recipe perhaps has the strongest Indo-Portuguese flavour. Sorpotel, as it is known in Goa, is traditionally cooked with heart, brain and fresh pig's blood added to the pork and liver. I admit to being faint-hearted and use only pork and liver but, instead of the fresh blood, I sometimes add black pudding, which you can try if you wish. Simply slice the black pudding, grill the slices and add at the end of cooking time. In Goa, a potent liquor known as feni, made from the fermented sap of the coconut palm tree is used in this recipe. I have used gin which works well.

Serves 4

450g/1lb boned shoulder
   or knuckle end of pork
250g/9oz pig's liver
2 x 5cm/2in pieces of
   cinnamon stick, halved
1 teaspoon black peppercorns
8 cloves
2.5cm/1in piece root ginger,
   sliced
4 large garlic cloves, bruised
2 teaspoons ground cumin
2 teaspoons ground coriander
½–1 teaspoon chilli powder
½ teaspoon ground turmeric
½ teaspoon ground cinnamon
½ teaspoon ground cloves
5 tablespoons cider vinegar
4 tablespoons sunflower
   or light olive oil
2.5cm/1in piece root ginger,
   finely grated or 1½ teaspoons
   ginger purée
4 large garlic cloves, crushed
   to a pulp or 2 teaspoons
   garlic purée
1 medium onion, chopped
2–4 green chillies, sliced
   lengthwise (seeded, if wished)
1 teaspoon salt
3 tablespoons gin

Put the pork and liver into a large saucepan and add 600ml/1pint water. Place over a high heat and bring to the boil. Skim off any scum and add the cinnamon, black peppercorns, cloves, ginger and garlic. Reduce the heat to low, cover the pan and simmer for 25–30 minutes.

Remove the meat and liver with a slotted spoon and let them cool. Strain the stock and set aside. When the meat and liver are cold enough to handle, cut them into bite-sized pieces. Combine the six dried spices in a bowl and add the vinegar to make a paste.

Heat the oil in a large pan over a medium heat and fry the pork and liver until browned. Add the spice paste, reduce the heat to low and fry for 2–3 minutes stirring all the time.

Add the ginger, garlic, onion, green chillies and salt. Raise the heat to medium, add the gin and fry for 2–3 minutes then add half the stock. Cook for 2–3 minutes and add the remaining stock. Continue to cook for a further 2–3 minutes and pour in 250ml/9fl oz warm water. Bring to the boil, cover the pan tightly and reduce the heat to low. Simmer for about 20 minutes or until the meat is tender. Remove from the heat and serve with Steamed Rice Cakes (page 75).

Prawn pickle

This popular pickle, known as Prawn Balchao, is absolutely divine. Prawns are preserved in asafoetida and turmeric with the distinctive flavours of garlic and chillies. Cider vinegar is used instead of traditional Goan vinegar. The pickle will last for up to six months in a screw-top jar provided you drain the prawns well – the absence of moisture is the secret of success.

Makes about 400g/14oz

1½ teaspoons salt
400g/14oz fresh cooked
    or defrosted and drained
    peeled prawns
125ml/4fl oz vegetable oil
½ teaspoon black mustard
    seeds
large pinch of asafoetida
2 teaspoons ground turmeric
10 large garlic cloves, minced
2.5cm/1in piece root ginger,
    finely grated
1–3 teaspoons chilli powder
1 teaspoon ground cumin
125ml/4fl oz cider vinegar

Add one teaspoon of the salt to the prawns and tie them up in a muslin cloth. Place in a colander over a bowl. Put a weight on top of the prawns and leave to drain for 1 hour.

Heat the oil over a medium heat and when it is hot, but not smoking, add the mustard seeds followed by the asafoetida and turmeric and immediately add the garlic and ginger. Reduce the heat to low and sauté them for about 2 minutes.

Add the drained prawns, chilli powder and cumin. Increase the heat slightly and stir-fry for 4–5 minutes or until all the moisture evaporates and the oil begins to float on the surface. Add the vinegar and the remaining salt then remove from the heat.

Let the pickle go completely cold and store in a sterilised, airtight jar in a cool dry place. Allow 3–4 weeks to mature. The pickle will keep well for at least six months and does not need refrigeration, but avoid using a wet spoon or leaving the jar open.

Great Indian Feasts

Hot and spicy chicken in mellow coconut cream

Chicken Cafreal, as it is known in Goa, is a superbly flavoured dish in which the spiciness is balanced by coconut cream. The climate in Goa is ideal for growing coconut, hence the extensive use of this versatile fruit in the region's cuisine. Here, I have used creamed coconut which comes in a block and is available in most supermarkets.

Serves 4

½ teaspoon black peppercorns
2–6 dried red chillies, roughly chopped
1 teaspoon cumin seeds
1 teaspoon coriander seeds
5cm/2in piece of cinnamon stick, broken up
seeds of 5 green cardamom pods
4 cloves
2.5cm/1in piece root ginger, finely grated or 1½ teaspoons ginger purée
4 large garlic cloves, crushed to a pulp or 1½ teaspoons garlic purée
juice of 1 lime
700g/1½lb skinned chicken thighs on the bone
1 teaspoon salt
3–4 tablespoons sunflower or vegetable oil
1 large onion, finely chopped
90g/3oz creamed coconut, cut into small pieces
2–3 tablespoons roughly chopped fresh coriander leaves
boiled basmati rice, to serve

Using a coffee or spice mill, grind the whole spices until they are fine and mix them with the ginger, garlic and lime juice to make a thick paste.

Put the chicken in a non-metallic bowl and add the spice paste and salt. Mix until the pieces are thoroughly coated with the spice paste, cover the bowl and refrigerate for 4–6 hours or overnight. Bring the chicken to room temperature before cooking.

In a heavy-based saucepan, heat half the oil over a medium heat and add the chicken. Fry for 2–3 minutes, stirring and cover the pan and reduce the heat to low. Let the chicken cook in its own juices for about 20 minutes then raise the heat to medium and continue to cook, stirring frequently until the cooking juices reduce to a paste-like consistency.

In a separate pan, heat the remaining oil over a medium heat and fry the onion until it is soft but not brown, about 5 minutes. Add the chicken, coconut and 250ml/9fl oz warm water. Bring to the boil, then reduce the heat to low and stir until the coconut is dissolved. Cover the pan and simmer for 5–6 minutes. Stir in the coriander leaves and remove from the heat. Serve with boiled basmati rice.

Mridula Baljekar

Coconut pancakes

Coconut Pancakes or Ale Belle is a classic example of the intermingling of Portuguese and Indian cultures. The batter for the pancake is more western than Indian with the exception of the use of coconut milk. The pancakes are traditionally served with a sauce made from sweetened coconut milk. To cut the richness, I have used lime juice and the zest of both lime and orange.

Serves 4

FOR THE PANCAKES
300ml/½ pint coconut milk
25g/1oz butter, melted
2 medium eggs, beaten
125g/4oz self-raising flour
½ teaspoon ground nutmeg
pinch of salt
sunflower oil, for frying

FOR THE SAUCE
90g/3oz caster sugar
finely grated zest and juice
   of 1 lime
finely grated zest of 1 orange
15g/½oz seedless raisins
90g/3oz creamed coconut,
   grated
2 tablespoons brandy
   (optional)

In a mixing bowl, blend the coconut milk and the butter. Gradually stir in the beaten eggs.

Sieve the flour into a bowl and stir in the nutmeg and salt. Add 1 tablespoon at a time of the dry mixture to the coconut milk mixture and beat well with a wire whisk between each addition. Alternatively, blend all the ingredients together in a blender or food processor. Let the batter stand for 20–25 minutes.

Pour 1 teaspoon oil into a 15–18cm/6–7in non-stick frying pan and place over a medium heat. Measure out 4 tablespoons of the batter into a cup and pour into the greased pan and spread it quickly. Allow to cook for 30 seconds and flip the pancake over. Cook for 30 seconds and fold it into a triangle and transfer to an oven-proof plate. Continue to cook and fold until you have made 8 pancakes. Keep the pancakes wrapped in foil in a warm oven while you make the sauce.

Put the sugar into a small saucepan and add 300ml/½ pint water. Bring to the boil and reduce the heat to medium and add the remaining ingredients except the coconut and brandy. Cook for 6–7 minutes and add the coconut, reduce the heat to low and simmer for 4–5 minutes. Stir in the brandy, if using, and remove from the heat.

Place 2 pancakes per person on individual serving plates and divide the sauce equally among them.

Creamy sago with raspberry coulis

Creamy Sago (Sabu Dane Che Alone) is a traditional recipe in which the sago is cooked in full-fat milk and coconut cream with nuts and spices. As it is quite rich, I like to accompany it with a raspberry coulis.

Serves 4–5

125g/4oz sago or tapioca
25g/1oz ghee or unsalted
   butter
3 cloves
2.5cm/1in piece of cinnamon
   stick
25g/1oz raw cashew pieces
25g/1oz seedless raisins
300ml/½pint full-fat milk
150ml/¼pint hot water
90g/3oz creamed coconut,
   cut into small pieces
90–125g/3–4oz caster sugar

FOR THE SAUCE
450g/1lb fresh or frozen
   raspberries
125g/4oz caster sugar
2 tablespoons Malibu
   (optional)

To make the sauce, put the raspberries and sugar in a saucepan and place over a high heat. Add 150ml/¼pint water and stir until the sugar has dissolved. Purée in a blender, then push the mixture through a sieve. Discard the seeds. Mix the sauce with the Malibu (if using). The sauce can be made 2–3 days in advance and stored in the fridge. It freezes well too.

Rinse the sago or tapioca and soak in cold water for 10–15 minutes.

In a non-stick saucepan, melt the ghee or butter over a low heat and add the cloves, cinnamon, cashews and raisins. Fry them gently until the cashews begin to brown and the raisins are puffed.

Add the milk, water and coconut. Stir over a medium heat until the coconut is dissolved, then drain the sago or tapioca and add. Cook until the mixture thickens. Stir constantly towards the end to ensure that the thickened mixture does not stick to the bottom of the pan. When the mixture stops sticking to the bottom and sides of the pan, the dessert is ready. This will take 10–12 minutes.

Put into individual ramekins or a decorative mould. Leave at room temperature for at least an hour, then unmould and drizzle the sauce over and around the dessert.

Mridula Baljekar

Durga Puja

Durga Puja is celebrated all over India, and is the biggest festival in the state of Bengal. It takes place in the autumn, and in Kolkata (formerly Calcutta), it is celebrated with such vim and vigour that the city is besieged by festivities, closing schools and businesses for nine days. The festival is devoted to the Goddess Durga, who in Hindu mythology is depicted as one of many forms of Goddess Parvati, the wife of Shiva, the destroyer. The power of Ma Durga, or Mother Goddess, is said to be greater than that of all Gods. She is portrayed as Shakti, or strength of the Hindu holy trinity of Lord Brahma, the Creator, Lord Vishnu, the Preserver, and Lord Shiva, the Destroyer. Ma Durga is supposed to be the destroyer of evil and it is to acknowledge her triumph over the wicked demon Mahisasur that Durga Puja is celebrated.

Beautifully painted clay images of the Goddess are constructed, and placed at the altar in temples where she is worshipped every day for nine days. Each day, prasad (holy offerings) are placed at the altar and after the rituals they are distributed to everyone present. Among the food items offered at the altar are Deep-fried Puffed Bread with Aromatic Potatoes, Fragrant Pigeon Peas and different kinds of sweets; no garlic or onion is used for the food that is offered to the Goddess. During the ten-day festivities, the first six days are devoted to religious ceremonies performed by the priest. On the seventh day, community spirit rises high and festivities begin with the placing of large platters of sweets and fruits as prasad in front of the Goddess. The three sacred foods, i.e., fresh coconut, bananas and raw rice must feature in the platters, along with the other items and these are then placed at the altar. A community lunch follows the ceremony on this day. Old, young, rich and poor try to forget their differences and devote the day to spreading the spirit of good will. On the eighth and the ninth days, families feast on delicious meat, fish, seafood and chicken dishes. Bengali housewives excel themselves in creating a feast table to be remembered throughout the year. On the tenth day, sweets are exchanged among friends and families. On the tenth day, which is supposedly the day Ma Durga defeated the demon, her images, worshipped at different locations, are taken through the illuminated streets with music being played loudly, and then immersed in the river. The spirit of the Goddess is said to then depart from her images.

Cultural and literary activities also flourish during Durga Puja. It is considered a good omen to launch a new play or a new book during this period. Evenings are spent in performing and watching singing and dancing.

Durga Puja is also celebrated in other parts of India, but the exuberance displayed by the Bengalis is the most notable in the country.

83

Mridula Baljekar

Deep-fried puffed bread

These are known as luchis in east and north-east India and as puris elsewhere in the country. You can use plain or wholemeal flour. I have chosen plain flour for this recipe in keeping with tradition in my part of the country. No raising agent is used for this bread.

Makes 16

275g/10oz plain flour, plus a
   little extra for dusting
½ teaspoon salt
¼ teaspoon sugar
1 tablespoon butter,
   margarine or ghee
175ml/6fl oz lukewarm water
sunflower oil, for deep frying

Sieve the flour into a large bowl and mix in the salt and sugar. Next, rub in the butter, margarine or ghee. Gradually add the lukewarm water and mix until a stiff dough is formed. Transfer the dough to a flat surface and knead it until it is soft and pliable. Alternatively, make the dough in a food processor, but mix the dry ingredients first. In either case, once the dough is made, cover it with a damp cloth and allow to rest for 20–30 minutes.

Divide the dough into two equal parts and make 8 equal-sized balls out of each. Flatten the balls into flat cakes by rotating them between your palms then pressing them down. Cover them with a damp cloth.

Heat the oil in a wok or large frying pan over a medium–high heat. Dust each flattened cake in the flour and roll out to 7.5cm/3in-diameter circles, taking care not to tear or pierce them as they will not puff up if damaged.

When the oil has a faint shimmer of rising smoke on the surface, carefully drop in one luchi and as soon as it floats, gently tap round the edges to encourage puffing. When it has puffed up, turn it over and fry the other side until browned. Drain on kitchen paper. Keep the fried luchis on a tray in a single layer.

COOK'S TIP
The bread is best eaten fresh, though they can be reheated briefly (3–4 minutes) in a hot oven. They are served with a spiced potato dish during religious ceremonies, but they are also perfect with any meat or poultry dish.

Monkfish in creamy cashew nut sauce

Bengali cuisine is renowned for its skilful cooking styles using fish and seafood. The Bay of Bengal provides an abundance of fish, and most of the population in the state lives on a daily diet of fish curry and rice. During celebrations and special occasions the curries are given a luxuriously festive touch. This is one such dish and is cooked in the korma style. You need a firm-fleshed fish – instead of monkfish, you could also use tilapia, salmon or even large prawns. In Bengal, they always use mustard oil which is very pungent, but you can use sunflower or light olive oil if you prefer.

Mridula Baljekar

Serves 4

700g/1½lb monkfish fillets
1 teaspoon ground turmeric
1 teaspoon salt
4 tablespoons sunflower or light olive oil
2.5cm/1in piece of cinnamon stick
4 green cardamom pods
1 large onion, finely chopped
2.5cm/1in piece root ginger, finely grated or 2 teaspoons ginger purée
1–3 green chillies, finely chopped (seeded, if wished)
90g/3oz roasted cashews
150ml/5fl oz single cream
2 tablespoons lemon juice
Cardamom-scented Basmati Rice (page 133), to serve

Wash the fish fillets gently and pat dry. Cut them into 5cm/2in chunks and lay them on a plate in a single layer. Sprinkle half the turmeric and half the salt over them and mix gently.

In a non-stick frying pan, heat half the oil over a medium-high heat and brown the pieces of fish quickly then drain on kitchen paper.

Wipe the pan clean and heat the remaining oil over a low heat. Add the cinnamon and cardamom and let them sizzle for 15–20 seconds until the cardamom pods have puffed up. Add the onion, ginger and green chillies and fry over a medium heat until the onion is soft and a pale golden colour (10–12 minutes). Stir regularly.

Meanwhile, purée the cashews with the cream. When the onion is ready, stir in the remaining turmeric followed by the cashew nut purée. Pour in 175ml/6fl oz warm water and add the remaining salt. Stir and lay the fish on the sauce in a single layer. Cover the pan tightly and cook over a low heat for 2–3 minutes.

Carefully spoon some of the sauce over the fish, shake the pan gently from side to side and re-cover. Cook for 1–2 minutes. Gently mix in the lemon juice, remove from the heat and serve with Cardamom-scented Basmati Rice.

Aromatic potatoes

When these potatoes are used as a holy offering with Deep-fried Puffed Bread, no onion or garlic is used, as both of these ingredients are believed to be stimulants. The Hindu religion dictates that during holy rituals one's mind should be void of all temptations. Pre-boiled potatoes are flavoured with just a few whole spices, but the combination can be varied to suit your taste.

Serves 4

2 tablespoons sunflower or
   light olive oil
½ teaspoon black mustard
   seeds
½ teaspoon cumin seeds
½ teaspoon fennel seeds
¼ teaspoon fenugreek seeds
1–2 dried red chillies,
   roughly chopped
½ teaspoon ground turmeric
750g/1½lb cold boiled
   potatoes, peeled and cut
   into bite-sized pieces
½ teaspoon salt
1 tablespoon sesame seeds

In a wok, heat the oil over a medium heat. When quite hot, but not smoking, add the mustard seeds. As soon as they start crackling, add the cumin and fennel followed by the fenugreek and red chillies. Stir in the turmeric and add the potatoes and salt. Stir to mix well and allow the potatoes to heat through.

Add the sesame seeds and cook, stirring, for 1–2 minutes. Remove from the heat and serve.

Great Indian Feasts

Crisp-fried aubergine

This is one of those side dishes that the people of Bengal and Assam in east and north-east India eat almost on a daily basis and it is never omitted from a festive menu. It is easy to make and is totally addictive! Make sure the oil is smoking hot, otherwise the aubergine will become soggy. Choose large aubergines with an unblemished, glossy skin.

Serves 4

50g/2oz chick pea flour
  (besan), sieved
1 tablespoon cornmeal,
  semolina or ground rice
½ teaspoon aniseeds
½ teaspoon cumin seeds
½ teaspoon onion seeds
  (kalonji)
½ teaspoon hot chilli powder
  or to taste
1 tablespoon white poppy
  seeds
½ teaspoon salt
2 tablespoons coriander
  leaves, finely chopped
1 large or 2 small aubergines
  (450g/1lb total weight)
sunflower oil, for deep frying

In a large mixing bowl, mix the chick pea flour with the remaining ingredients except the aubergines and the oil.

Halve the aubergines lengthways and slice them into approximately 5mm/¼in thick slices. Rinse them in cold water and shake off excess water and let some of the water cling to the slices. Add them to the spiced chick pea flour and mix them by tossing and turning and sprinkling a little water if necessary so that the aubergine slices are coated with the spiced flour.

Heat the oil in a wok or other suitable pan for deep frying. When the oil has reached at least 180°C/350°F or a small cube of one-or-two-day-old bread dropped in the oil floats immediately to the surface, start adding one slice of aubergine at a time until you have a full, single layer without overcrowding the pan. Fry the aubergine until crisp and golden brown. Drain on kitchen paper.

Mridula Baljekar

Toffee-flavoured baked yogurt dessert

The inspiration for this recipe came from a traditional Bengali dish called Misti Doi. Misti in Bengali means sweet and Doi is yogurt. It is sold in all sweet shops and street stalls in Bengal in earthenware pots and is pure ambrosia! This is a quick method, based on a more modern version which I came across recently. The use of condensed milk has given it a wickedly delicious toffee flavour. When I feel like letting go, I serve it with extra toffee sauce! For a healthier version, serve with your favourite fresh fruits. The dessert keeps well in the fridge for up to 7 days.

Mridula Baljekar

Serves 4–5

150g/5oz whole milk plain
   yogurt
400g/14oz evaporated milk
400g/14oz condensed milk
½ teaspoon ground
   cardamom
¼ teaspoon freshly grated
   nutmeg
melted butter, for greasing
pistachio nuts, to decorate

Preheat the oven to 180°C/350°F/Gas Mark 4.

Put the yogurt in a large bowl and beat with a wire whisk until smooth. Add the evaporated milk and beat again. Next, add the condensed milk. ground cardamom and nutmeg and continue to beat until all the ingredients are well blended.

Brush a 23cm/9in square baking dish with a little melted butter and pour the mixture into it. Bake for 30–40 minutes or until lightly set. Cool and chill for 1–2 hours and cut into squares.

Meanwhile, preheat the grill to medium. Grill the pistachio nuts until lightly browned, then cool and crush them. Sprinkle the crushed nuts on top of the dessert and serve.

COOK'S TIPS
As an alternative the pudding can be baked in shallow individual bowls for about 20 minutes. Instead of grilling the nuts they can be roasted in the oven during the last 12–15 minutes when the dessert is being baked.

Festive split chick peas with aromatic spices

Split chick peas or channa dhal is available from Indian grocers. Here, the natural earthy flavour and the nutty taste of split chick peas are intensified by the added warmth of cinnamon and the sweet, aromatic taste of green cardamom pods. Split chick peas are also packed full of protein and fibre. You could use yellow split peas instead, but they don't taste quite the same. This is a festive dish, hence the use of ghee or butter, but you could use oil if you prefer.

Serves 4–5

225g/8oz split chick peas
50g/2oz ghee or unsalted butter
2 x 2.5cm/1in pieces of cinnamon stick
6 green cardamom pods, bruised
2 bay leaves
1 large onion, finely chopped
1–2 dried red chillies, roughly chopped
½ teaspoon ground turmeric
½ teaspoon chilli powder
1 teaspoon salt
600ml/1 pint warm water
50g/2oz desiccated coconut
2 ripe tomatoes, skinned and chopped
2 tablespoons chopped fresh coriander leaves
rice or bread, to serve

Wash the split chick peas in several changes of water and soak them for 2–3 hours. Drain well.

Melt the ghee or butter over a low heat and add the cinnamon, cardamom and bay leaves. Let them sizzle for a few seconds until the cardamom pods are puffed.

Add the onion and red chillies and increase the heat to medium. Fry them until the onion is lightly browned (8–9 minutes), stirring regularly to ensure even browning.

Add the chick peas and stir-fry for 2–3 minutes then stir in the turmeric and chilli powder. Continue to stir-fry for a further minute or two then add the salt, warm water and coconut. Bring to the boil, cover the pan tightly and reduce the heat to low. Simmer for 35–40 minutes or until the chick peas are tender but not mushy.

Add the tomatoes, cook for about 1 minute and then stir in the coriander leaves. Remove from the heat and serve with any rice or bread.

Aromatic lamb and split chick pea stew

Tender cubes of lamb, aromatised with cinnamon, cloves and two types of cardamom and smothered in earthy split chick peas (channa dhal), produce truly sublime taste sensations. An added bonus here is the nutty taste of the chick peas.

Serves 4

175g/6oz split chick peas

4 tablespoons sunflower or light olive oil

2 x 5cm/2-in pieces of cinnamon stick, halved

3 dark brown cardamom pods, tops slightly peeled back (see Cook's Tip)

4 green cardamom pods, bruised

5 cloves

1 large onion, finely chopped

2.5cm/1in piece root ginger, finely grated or 2 teaspoons ginger purée

4–5 large garlic cloves, crushed to a pulp or 1 tablespoon garlic purée

2 teaspoons ground cumin

½ teaspoon ground turmeric

½–1 teaspoon chilli powder

450g/1lb lamb neck fillet, cut into 2.5cm/1in cubes

75g/3oz plain yogurt

1 teaspoon salt

1 tablespoon tomato purée

1 tablespoon ghee or unsalted butter

½ teaspoon garam masala

1 tablespoon chopped fresh coriander leaves

1 tablespoon chopped fresh mint leaves

Wash the chick peas in several changes of water and soak them for 2–3 hours. Drain well.

In a heavy-based saucepan, heat the oil over a low heat and add the cinnamon, both types of cardamom pods and the cloves. Sizzle gently for 25–30 seconds, then add the onion. Increase the heat to medium and fry the onion until soft (6–7 minutes), stirring regularly. Add the ginger and garlic and fry until the onion is lightly browned. Add the cumin, turmeric and chilli powder. Cook for about a minute and add the meat. Raise the heat to medium-high and stir-fry the meat for 2–3 minutes.

Beat the yogurt with a fork and add half of it to the meat. Continue to stir-fry for 2–3 minutes and add the remaining yogurt. Stir-fry for a further 2–3 minutes and add the salt and tomato purée. Pour in 600ml/1 pint warm water and bring to the boil. Reduce the heat to low, cover and simmer for 30–35 minutes.

Meanwhile, melt the ghee or butter in another pan over a low heat and add the drained chick peas. Raise the heat to medium high and stir-fry the chick peas for 4–5 minutes. Add the fried chick peas to the meat, stir and re-cover. Cook for 30–40 minutes or until the meat and the chick peas are tender. Stir in the garam masala, coriander leaves and mint and remove from the heat.

COOK'S TIP
You can buy large, dark brown cardamom pods from Indian grocers. Lamb dishes are complemented by these large pods. Using a small knife, open the top of each pod slightly, leaving the seeds intact to release flavour into the sauce.

Mridula Baljekar

Fragrant pigeon peas with seasonal vegetables

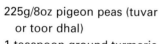

Pigeon peas (tuvar or toor dhal) are available in Indian stores. They generally have a glossy appearance because they are preserved in castor oil. You need to wash them thoroughly before cooking. You can use other varieties of lentils if you cannot get pigeon peas.

Serves 4

225g/8oz pigeon peas (tuvar or toor dhal)
1 teaspoon ground turmeric
2 green chillies, sliced lengthways
½ lemon, thickly sliced
1½ teaspoons salt
225g/8oz sweet potatoes, cut into bite-sized pieces
225g/8oz green beans, cut into 2.5cm/1in pieces
3 tablespoons sunflower oil
½ teaspoon black mustard seeds
½ teaspoon onion seeds (kalonji)
1 red onion, finely chopped
2.5cm/1in piece root ginger, grated or minced
1 green chilli, finely chopped
2 teaspoons ground cumin
1 teaspoon ground coriander
2 ripe tomatoes, skinned and chopped
2 tablespoons chopped fresh coriander leaves
plain boiled basmati rice, to serve

Wash the pigeon peas in several changes of water and put them into a saucepan with 1.1 litres/2 pints hot water. Add half the turmeric, the sliced green chillies and the sliced lemon. Bring to the boil, reduce the heat to low, cover and simmer for 15 minutes.

Add the salt, sweet potatoes and green beans. Bring back to the boil, cover and simmer for a further 15 minutes.

Heat the oil in a wok or large frying pan over a medium heat. When hot, but not smoking, add the mustard seeds followed by the onion seeds. Let them sizzle and crackle for 15–20 seconds and add the onion. Fry until the onion is light brown and add the ginger and chopped green chilli. Continue to fry until the onion is well browned and stir in the cumin and coriander followed by the remaining turmeric. Cook for about 30 seconds and stir in the tomatoes then add the contents of the wok to the cooked pigeon peas. Add the coriander leaves and remove from the heat. Serve with plain boiled basmati rice along with any meat or poultry dish of your choice.

Cardamom-scented chicken in poppy seed sauce

A typical festive dish from the state of Bengal, known as Murgi Posto. Take care while roasting the poppy seeds – you only need to roast them until they turn a shade darker. Remove them from the pan as soon as they change colour. If you leave them to cool in the hot pan, they will continue to darken which will impair both the appearance and taste of the dish.

Mridula Baljekar

Serves 4

750g/1½lb chicken thigh
   fillets, skinned and cut
   into halves
¼ teaspoon turmeric
½ teaspoon salt
2 tablespoons lemon juice
25g/1oz white poppy seeds
2–3 tablespoons sunflower
   oil
6 green cardamom pods,
   bruised
2.5cm/1in piece of cinnamon
   stick, halved
2 bay leaves
1 large onion, finely chopped
2.5cm/1in piece root ginger,
   finely grated or 2 teaspoons
   ginger purée
4–5 large garlic cloves,
   crushed to a pulp or
   2 teaspoons garlic purée
½–1 teaspoon hot chilli powder
   made into a paste with a
   little water or ½–1 teaspoon
   red chilli paste
½ teaspoon salt
1 teaspoon sugar
250ml/9fl oz warm water
chopped fresh coriander
   leaves, to garnish

Put the chicken in a non-metallic bowl and add the turmeric, salt and lemon juice. Mix well and set aside for 30 minutes.

Preheat a small heavy-based saucepan or skillet over a medium heat and add the poppy seeds. Stir them around for a minute or two until they go a shade darker. Remove from the pan to cool, then grind them in a coffee mill.

Heat the oil and add the cardamom, cinnamon and bay leaves. Let them sizzle for 25–30 seconds and add the onion. Fry until the onion is soft (5–7 minutes) and add the ginger and garlic. Continue to fry until the onion is brown. Add the chilli paste and the chicken. Increase the heat to medium-high and stir-fry the chicken for 2–3 minutes. Add the salt, sugar and warm water, cover and simmer for 10–12 minutes.

Add the ground roasted poppy seeds and simmer, covered, until chicken is tender. Add 1–2 tablespoons warm water to prevent the thickened sauce sticking to the bottom of the pan. Garnish with fresh coriander and serve with plain boiled basmati rice.

Onam

In Kerala, the spice coast of India, Onam is a major festival. In practical terms it marks the end of the south-west monsoons, but India is a place where legends and myths play a strong part in the lives of its people. Legend has it that Onam is celebrated in honour of King Mahabali who once ruled Kerala. He was depicted as a good king who was renowned for his kindness to his subjects. When he was ousted by Lord Vishnu, Mahabli expressed his desire to visit his land once a year which was granted. Onam is therefore celebrated both to commemorate the happy time under Mahabali's rule and his return once a year to visit his people.

A few days prior to Onam, householders clean their houses and decorate them. Outside each house, a flower mat, known in the local language as pookalam, is placed. New clothes are bought for the entire family.

A dazzling fireworks display and a colourful procession of elephants are among the highlights of this festival. The popular Indian dance Kathakali, which originated in Kerala, is performed in the evening.

Another attractive feature during Onam is a boat race known locally as Vallamkali. Several hundred men row the boats to the beat of drums. A silk parasol is placed above each boat from which gold coins are hung. The long snakelike boats make a spectacular sight.

Onam is one festival which seems to unite all races and religions. It is celebrated with great enthusiasm by Hindus, Muslims and Christians alike.

The fun and games of snake-boat races and other celebrations reach a climax with an elaborate feast in every family. The sumptuous meal is generally served on banana leaves. As fish and seafood are available in abundance on the vast coastline, the centre of attraction of this meal is a fish and/or seafood dish cooked in coconut milk, which is also plentiful in the area. A chutney is also made with coconut, yogurt and spices, there are plenty of vegetable dishes, and the staple food, rice. The dessert also contains rice – it is an Indian rice pudding known as Payasam.

Mridula Baljekar

Pineapple with coconut, curry leaves and chillies

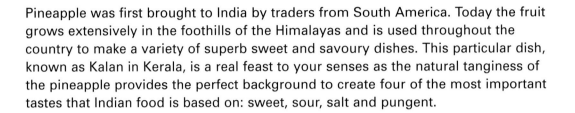

Pineapple was first brought to India by traders from South America. Today the fruit grows extensively in the foothills of the Himalayas and is used throughout the country to make a variety of superb sweet and savoury dishes. This particular dish, known as Kalan in Kerala, is a real feast to your senses as the natural tanginess of the pineapple provides the perfect background to create four of the most important tastes that Indian food is based on: sweet, sour, salt and pungent.

Serves 4

1 small pineapple
½ teaspoon ground turmeric
1 teaspoon salt
25–50g/1–2oz granulated
  sugar
25g/1oz desiccated coconut
1–3 long slim dried red
  chillies, torn into pieces
2 ripe, firm bananas, cut into
1cm/½in thick slices
2 tablespoons sunflower oil
½ teaspoon black mustard
  seeds
1 green chilli, seeded and
  finely chopped
12–15 fresh or dried curry
  leaves

Peel the pineapple and remove the 'eyes' with a small sharp knife. Cut it into 8 boat-shaped pieces and remove the central core from each piece. Cut into 1cm/½in wedges and put into a saucepan with the turmeric, salt and sugar. Add 450ml/16fl oz water, cover and cook over a medium heat until the pineapple is tender (15–20 minutes).

Meanwhile, grind the coconut and the red chillies in a coffee grinder and add to the cooked pineapple. Stir in the bananas and remove from the heat.

In a small saucepan or a steel ladle, heat the oil over medium heat. When hot, switch off the heat and add the mustard seeds followed by the green chilli and curry leaves. Stir the flavoured oil with the mustard seeds, chilli and curry leaves into the cooked pineapple and serve.

Rose and saffron-scented rice dessert

Payasam, a traditional rice pudding, is placed as a religious offering in front of the altar in temples during Onam. Once the prayers are over, it is served as a dessert. This is a quick version, using canned rice pudding. You save all the time and still get to eat an enduring dessert!

Serves 4

a good pinch of saffron
   threads, pounded
125ml/4fl oz hot milk
25g/1oz ghee or unsalted
   butter
6 green cardamom pods,
   bruised
2.5cm/1in piece of cinnamon
   stick
750g/1½lb can of creamed
   rice
2–3 tablespoons double
   cream
1–2 tablespoons caster sugar
1 tablespoon rose water
1 tablespoon shelled,
   unsalted pistachio nuts
washed fresh rose petals,
   to decorate

Soak the pounded saffron in the milk and set aside.

Melt the ghee or butter gently over a low heat and add the cardamom and cinnamon. Let them sizzle until the cardamom pods are puffed.

Add the creamed rice and saffron milk. Bring it to a slow simmer and add the cream and sugar. Let it bubble gently for 5 minutes, then remove from the heat and set aside to cool. To speed this up, stand the pan in a bowl of iced water. When cold, stir in the rose water.

Preheat the grill to medium and toast the pistachio nuts. Cool, then crush them. Sprinkle over the dessert and serve decorated with the rose petals.

Tiger prawns in coconut and tamarind sauce

This is known as Pappas and is the central attraction during important festive occasions such as Onam. Locally caught large fresh prawns are cooked in a luxurious coconut sauce tinged with turmeric and speckled with mustard seeds.

Serves 4

1 tablespoon coriander seeds
2–6 dried red chillies, torn
  into small pieces
½ teaspoon black peppercorns
4 tablespoons sunflower
  or vegetable oil
½ teaspoon black mustard
  seeds
6 fenugreek seeds
1 large onion, finely chopped
2.5cm/1in piece root ginger,
  grated
4–5 garlic cloves, crushed
1–3 green chillies, chopped
  (seeded if wished)
450g/1lb cooked and peeled
  tiger prawns (thawed and
  drained if frozen)
1 teaspoon salt
125ml/4fl oz canned coconut
  milk
10–12 fresh curry leaves
1 tablespoon tamarind juice
  or 1½ tablespoons lime
  juice
boiled basmati rice, to serve

Grind the coriander seeds, red chillies and peppercorns in a coffee grinder until fine.

Heat the oil over a medium heat and add the mustard seeds. Immediately follow with the fenugreek seeds and the onion, ginger, garlic and green chillies. Fry until the onions are a light golden colour (10–12 minutes), stirring regularly.

Add the ground ingredients and sauté for 1–2 minutes, then add the prawns and the salt.

Add the coconut milk to the prawns. Add the curry leaves and simmer gently, uncovered, for 5–6 minutes.

Stir in the tamarind or lime juice and remove from the heat. Serve with boiled basmati rice.

Mridula Baljekar

Shredded cabbage with coconut

A quick and easy recipe, known as Thoren in Kerala, which can be served as an accompaniment to any meat, poultry or fish dish.

Serves 4

2 tablespoons sunflower
  or vegetable oil
½ teaspoon black mustard
  seeds
2.5cm/1in piece root ginger,
  grated
1–3 green chillies, seeded and
  cut into julienne strips
6–8 fresh or dried curry leaves
450g/1lb green or white
  cabbage, finely shredded
1–2 carrots, coarsely grated
25g/1oz unsweetened
  desiccated coconut
1 teaspoon salt

Heat the oil in a wok or frying pan over a low heat. When hot, add the mustard seeds and, as soon as they pop, add the ginger, chillies and curry leaves. Cook gently for 1 minute, stirring.

Add the cabbage, carrots, coconut and salt. Stir and sprinkle over 3 tablespoons water. Cover the pan and cook for 10 minutes or until the vegetables are cooked but al dente. Remove from the heat and serve.

Mridula Baljekar

Mixed vegetables in coconut sauce

No major festival feast in Kerala is complete without this divine mixed vegetable curry known as Avial. During Diwali and Onam, Avial is served on banana leaves with Prawn or Fish Pappas (see page 101) and boiled basmati rice.

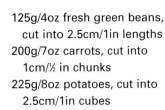

Serves 4–5

125g/4oz fresh green beans, cut into 2.5cm/1in lengths
200g/7oz carrots, cut into 1cm/½in chunks
225g/8oz potatoes, cut into 2.5cm/1in cubes
5–6 baby aubergines, quartered lengthways or 1 small aubergine (200g/7oz approx), quartered lengthways and cut into 2.5 cm/1in pieces
5–6 shallots, halved
½ teaspoon ground turmeric
½ teaspoon chilli powder
1 teaspoon salt
2 teaspoons cumin seeds
50g/2oz unsweetened desiccated coconut
175g/6oz whole milk plain yogurt
1 unripe banana, peeled and cut into 1cm/½in chunks
3–4 green chillies, quartered lengthways (seeded if wished)
6–8 fresh or dried curry leaves
boiled basmati rice, to serve

Put all the vegetables together into a large pan and add 350ml/12fl oz hot water. Add the turmeric, chilli powder and salt. Bring to the boil, reduce the heat to low and cover the pan. Cook for 8–10 minutes or until the vegetables are tender, but still firm (except the aubergine, which will be soft).

Meanwhile, preheat a small heavy pan over a medium heat. When hot, dry roast the cumin seeds for 30–40 seconds until they release their aroma. Remove from the heat and transfer the seeds to a plate and cool slightly.

Grind the coconut and the roasted cumin seeds in a coffee grinder. Beat the yogurt until smooth and beat in the coconut mixture.

When the vegetables are ready, remove the pan from the heat and allow to cool for 2–3 minutes. Gradually stir in the yogurt mixture and add the banana, green chillies and curry leaves. Return the pan to a very low heat and let the contents bubble gently for 4–5 minutes. Remove from the heat, and let the curry stand, covered, for 5–6 minutes. Serve with boiled basmati rice.

Coconut chutney

In Kerala, this chutney will, of course, be made with fresh coconut. I have used desiccated coconut here, but fresh coconut is also easily available in supermarkets these days though it is laborious to extract the flesh. This chutney is a hot favourite with Spiced Potato-filled Rice pancakes (page 18) and Steamed Semolina Cakes (page 21).

Serves 4

90g/3oz desiccated coconut
2 tablespoons sunflower oil
1–2 dried red chillies, chopped
1–2 fresh green chillies, chopped
1 teaspoon channa dhal or yellow split peas
½ teaspoon salt
½ teaspoon sugar
1½ tablespoons lemon juice
½ teaspoon black mustard seeds

Put the coconut in a heatproof bowl and pour in enough boiling water to just cover it. Set aside for 10–12 minutes.

Heat two teaspoons of the oil in a small wok or steel ladle over a medium heat and add both types of chillies and the channa dhal or yellow split peas. Let them sizzle for a few seconds and switch off the heat source.

Put the undrained coconut into a blender and add the fried spices, salt, sugar and lemon juice. Blend until smooth and transfer to a serving bowl.

Heat the remaining oil in a small wok or steel ladle over a medium heat. When hot, throw in the mustard seeds. Allow them to crackle then pour over the chutney. Serve at room temperature. This chutney is best eaten fresh.

Fish in ginger–coconut sauce with crisp-fried curry leaves

The cuisine of Kerala is light and refreshing, using locally grown coconut and exotic spices. The food is generally healthy with minimum use of fat and maximum use of fresh ingredients. A huge variety of fish and seafood gives Kerala's cuisine that special taste and flavour. This dish, known as Meen Molee, is delicious with steamed basmati rice. I have used tilapia here, but you can use any firm-fleshed fish.

Serves 4

1 teaspoon salt
juice of 1 lemon
450g/1lb tilapia fillets,
    cut into 2.5cm/1in cubes
4 tablespoons sunflower oil
1 large onion, finely chopped
2 green chillies, chopped
    (seeded, if liked)
5cm/2in piece root ginger,
    finely grated or 1½
    tablespoons ginger purée
4 large garlic cloves, crushed
    to a pulp or 1 tablespoon
    garlic purée
1 teaspoon ground cumin
1 tablespoon ground
    coriander
½ teaspoon ground turmeric
½ teaspoon chilli powder
400ml/14fl oz canned
    coconut milk
½ teaspoon black mustard
    seeds
10–12 fresh or dried curry
    leaves
steamed basmati rice, to
    serve

Sprinkle half the salt and lemon juice over the fish and set aside.

Heat 3 tablespoons of the oil and sauté the onions and chillies until the onion is soft. Add the ginger and garlic and continue to cook until the onion is light brown.

Add the cumin, coriander, turmeric and chilli powder. Cook for a minute or two and add the coconut milk, fish and the remaining salt. Simmer gently for 5–6 minutes.

Meanwhile, heat the remaining oil in a small saucepan or a steel ladle over a medium heat. When the oil reaches smoking point, remove the pan from the heat and add the mustard seeds. As soon as they start crackling, add the curry leaves and fry them for about 30 seconds until crisp. Pour the entire contents into the pan in which the fish is being cooked. Stir gently and remove from the heat.

Spiced lentil broth

This spicy lentil broth (Rasam) is traditionally served with meals. It is also wonderful to drink as an appetiser in small cups.

Serves 4–5

90g/3oz split red lentils
    (masoor dhal)
½ teaspoon ground turmeric
4–5 large garlic cloves,
    crushed
4–5 shallots, chopped
25g/1oz unsweetened
    desiccated coconut
3–4 dried red chillies, torn
    into pieces
1 tablespoon coriander seeds
1 teaspoon cumin seeds
10–12 black peppercorns
8–10 fresh curry leaves
1½ teaspoons salt
¾ teaspoon tamarind
    concentrate or the juice
    of 1 lime
1 tablespoon finely chopped
    fresh coriander leaves

Wash the lentils in several changes of water and put into a saucepan with the turmeric, garlic, shallots and 1.1 litres/2 pints hot water. Place over a medium heat and let it come to a rolling boil.

Meanwhile, grind the coconut, chillies, coriander, cumin and peppercorns in a coffee grinder and add to the lentils. When the liquid has come to the boil, reduce the heat to low, partially cover the pan and simmer for 20 minutes.

Add the curry leaves, salt and tamarind or lime juice and simmer for a further 5–6 minutes. Check that the tamarind has dissolved completely.

Purée the lentils until smooth and return to the pan. Heat gently and stir in the coriander leaves. Serve hot.

Mustard and curry leaf-flavoured yogurt sauce

This sauce is comprised of just yogurt and spices, but the resulting taste and flavour definitely have the ability to lift your mood! In Kerala, it is known as Pulicherry and is served with boiled rice and other dry spiced dishes. The Pulicherry is served hot and is used to moisten the rice and it tastes divine. I also like to serve the sauce in shot glasses in between courses which goes down really well. If you do this, I would advise you to remove the curry leaves and the pieces of chillies before serving.

Serves 4

500g/½ kg whole milk plain yogurt
200ml/7 fl oz water
1 teaspoon sugar
1 teaspoon salt
2 tablespoons sunflower oil
1 teaspoon black mustard seeds
? teaspoon fenugreek seeds
2 large garlic cloves, crushed to a pulp
1cm/½ in piece of root ginger, finely grated
1-3 dried red chillies, scissor snipped
12-15 fresh curry leaves
½ teaspoon ground turmeric

Whisk the yogurt until smooth. This is very important as the yogurt will split during cooking if not whisked properly. Gradually add the water, sugar and salt and continue to whisk until well blended.

In a wok, or other suitable pan, heat the oil over a medium-high heat. When almost smoking, switch off the heat source and add the mustard seeds. Allow them to crackle for 5-10 seconds and add the fenugreek seeds followed by the remaining ingredients. Place the pan over a medium-low heat and sauté the ingredients for 1–2 minutes.

Add the diluted yogurt, reduce the heat to low and let it simmer very gently until the yogurt is heated through. Do not boil as high temperature will cause the yogurt to curdle. Remove from the heat and serve.

Mridula Baljekar

The Diwali Delights

Diwali is the biggest and the happiest of all Hindu festivals. Diwali takes place in the autumn over five days. It is celebrated to welcome the Hindu prince Rama from 14 years of exile. Rama was the reincarnation of the Hindu god Vishnu, and he was sentenced to 14 years in exile by his wicked stepmother who wanted her own son to become the king.

During Diwali, which is also known as the Festival of Lights, oil lamps are lit everywhere to welcome Rama, who was supposed to have returned in the evening. Hindus also worship Lakshmi, the Goddess of Wealth, as she reincarnated as Rama's wife Sita. To welcome Lakshmi, Indian homes have oil-lit lamps through to the early hours of the morning, as it is believed that she never enters a dark home.

When Rama was in exile, the demon king Ravana abducted his wife Sita, whom Rama then rescued from him. To celebrate this victory of good over evil, people made up straw effigies of Ravana filled with firecrackers and set them off, hence the tradition of fireworks during Diwali.

Before Diwali, another big festival, Dussera, is held. This marks the victory of Rama in rescuing his wife Sita. All kinds of meat dishes as well as alcohol are allowed during Dussera. It is a time to rejoice without any restrictions on food and drink.

The business community of northern India begin their new year on the fourth day of Diwali. They give gifts and bonuses to their employees.

Diwali is a festival when sweetmeats are the main food items. Exchanging sweets among families and friends is an ancient tradition and Hindus believe that sweets represent our inner goodness. Coconut treats are particularly popular, such as weet puffed parathas stuffed with coconut and spices, sweet samosas filled with coconut and pancakes filled with sweetened coconut.

Vegetarian food is the order of the day during Diwali because the Hindu religion is based on Ahimsa (non-violence), which means that you should not destroy another life for your own pleasure. A salad of soaked lentils with diced cucumber, grated coconut and lemon juice, said to be the favourite of the god Rama, is popular. Deep-fried savoury snacks made of chick pea flour or soaked and ground lentils are among other treats enjoyed during Diwali.

Mridula Baljekar

Preparing ground cardamom for Indian sweets

Most Indian sweets and sweet-meats use ground cardamom which is difficult to buy. If you grind it and do not use it within about a month the volatile oil will start to disappear and along with it will go all the flavour. You can overcome this problem by grinding the cardamom seeds with some of the sugar from the recipe in a coffee or spice mill. This will ensure maximum flavour. Alternatively, grind the seeds using a mortar and pestle, but do make sure you grind them finely. The third alternative is to grind the whole cardamom pods in a coffee or spice mill then sieve it so that you end up with only the fine powder. Store in an airtight container, away from direct light.

Festive coconut-filled pastries

These delicious morsels are a firm Diwali tradition in parts of southern India. To save time and effort I have used filo pastry and baked them, instead of the traditional method of deep-frying. In southern India these are made with freshly grated coconut, which has a richer taste, but I have used the desiccated variety and enriched it with evaporated milk.

Makes 12

60g/2½oz desiccated coconut
40g/1½oz light soft brown
    sugar
25g/1oz raw cashews, lightly
    crushed with a rolling pin
25g/1oz seedless raisins
250ml/9fl oz evaporated milk
½ teaspoon ground nutmeg
½ teaspoon ground cinnamon
12 sheets of filo pastry,
    approx 28 x 18cm/11 x 7in
melted butter, to brush over
    the pastry
icing sugar, to dust

Put the coconut, sugar, cashews, raisins and evaporated milk into a small, heavy-based saucepan and place over a medium heat. Stir and mix the ingredients thoroughly. As soon as the milk starts bubbling, reduce the heat to low and cook, uncovered, until the coconut has absorbed all the milk (8–10 minutes), stirring frequently.

Remove the pan from the heat and stir in the spices. Cool, then divide into 12 equal portions.

Preheat the oven to 180°C/350°F/Gas Mark 4. Line a baking sheet with greased greaseproof paper or non-stick baking parchment.

Next, place a sheet of filo pastry on a pastry board and brush well with some melted butter. Fold the pastry in half lengthwise. Brush with butter again and fold it widthwise.

Place a portion of the filling on one half of the pastry and fold the other half over it. Seal the edges with cold water. Press the edges with a fork and trim with a pair of scissors. Make the remaining pastries in the same way and place them on the prepared baking sheet. Brush them liberally with melted butter and bake in the centre of the oven for 20–25 minutes or until they are golden brown. Sprinkle them with sieved icing sugar, if liked, and serve hot or cold with tea or coffee.

Mridula Baljekar

Coconut-filled wheat pancakes

This is my mother's speciality, known as Pati Shapta in Assam and Bengal, which we always enjoyed during Diwali. She used a fresh coconut from the coconut tree in our garden. As I have neither such luxury nor the time she had at her disposal, I compromised with desiccated coconut! The pancakes are made with wholemeal flour, which lends a healthy and wholesome taste. The batter needs to rest for 30 minutes during which time you could make the filling.

Makes 6

FOR THE PANCAKES
2 medium eggs
150g/5oz wholemeal flour
1 teaspoon ground cinnamon
1 tablespoon caster sugar
200ml/7fl oz whole milk
   melted ghee or unsalted
   butter, for frying

FOR THE FILLING
50g/2oz desiccated coconut
50g/2oz soft dark brown
   sugar
25g/1oz raw cashews, lightly
   crushed with a rolling pin
250ml/9fl oz evaporated milk
1 teaspoon ground cardamom
whipped cream or ice cream,
   to serve

Put all the pancake ingredients, except the ghee or butter, in a large bowl and beat with a wire whisk until smooth. Alternatively, use a food processor or a blender. Set aside for 30 minutes.

Mix all the filling ingredients, except the ground cardamom, in a small saucepan and place over a medium heat. As soon as it begins to bubble, reduce the heat to low and let it simmer, uncovered, for 8–10 minutes, stirring occasionally.

Stir in the ground cardamom, remove the pan from the heat and allow the mixture to cool.

To cook the pancakes, place a non-stick or cast-iron frying pan over a low heat, when hot, spread about ½ teaspoon melted ghee or butter on it. Transfer about 2 tablespoons of the batter into a cup or small jug and pour it in the pan. You now have to be very quick and spread it by tilting the pan before the pancake has a chance to set. In a minute or so the pancake will set, let it cook for a further minute, then carefully turn it over with a thin spatula or toss it! Cook the other side for about a minute or until brown spots appear.

Spread about a tablespoon of the filling on one side of the pancake and roll it up. Make the rest of the pancakes the same way. You can serve them on their own with tea or coffee or with whipped cream or ice cream as a dessert.

Deep-fried milk balls in cardamom syrup

These are known as Gulab Jamoon and are traditionally made with khoya and chenna. Both of these are dairy products and one needs an abundance of time to make them. I have made them with full-cream dried milk powder, which you can buy from Asian shops. If you cannot find it, then use dried skimmed milk powder and single cream.

Makes 16

175g/6oz full-cream milk powder or dried skimmed milk powder
90g/3oz semolina
2 teaspoons plain flour
1 teaspoon ground cardamom
1 teaspoon baking powder
40g/1½oz ghee or unsalted butter, melted
150ml/¼ pint milk or single cream if using skimmed milk powder
1 teaspoon saffron threads soaked in 2 tablespoons hot milk
350g/12oz granulated sugar
850ml/1½ pints water
10 green cardamom pods, bruised
oil, for deep frying
150ml/5fl oz whipped double cream mixed with 2 tablespoons of rose water, to serve

In a large mixing bowl, combine the milk powder, semolina, plain flour, ground cardamom and baking powder. Add the ghee or butter and rub in until blended.

Add the milk or cream and the saffron threads along with the milk in which they were soaked. Mix until a soft dough is formed and knead it on a pastry board until smooth. Divide the dough into two equal parts and make 8 equal-sized balls out of each part. Rotate the balls between your palms to make the balls as smooth as possible without any surface cracks.

Put the sugar and water in a saucepan and bring to the boil. Stir until the sugar has dissolved. Add the cardamom pods and turn the heat down then simmer the syrup for 6–8 minutes. Remove from the heat.

Meanwhile, heat the oil in a karahi or wok over a low heat and deep-fry the milk balls (jamoons) gently until they are a rich dark-brown colour. When you first put them in the hot oil, they will sink. After a couple of minutes they will start floating in the oil, if they do not, gently ease them away from the base of the pan using a thin spatula. Turn them over once or twice until they brown.

Remove the jamoons with a slotted spoon and put them into the prepared syrup. Allow them to soak in the syrup while you fry the next batch. Leave them to soak in the syrup for a couple of hours before serving with rose-flavoured cream.

Spice-crusted mixed nuts

All kinds of dried fruit and nuts are synonymous with Diwali. They are gift-wrapped and given to friends and business associates. For me, Diwali would not be the same without nuts, and who can resist the temptation of a few fried or roasted nuts? They are even more irresistible when coated with a touch of spices.

Serves 8–10

150g/5oz shelled almonds
150g/5oz raw whole cashews
½ teaspoon garlic powder
4 tablespoons water
½–1 teaspoon chilli powder
2 teaspoons ground
   coriander
1 teaspoon ground cumin
25g/1oz chick pea flour
   (besan), sieved
oil, for deep-frying

Put the nuts in a mixing bowl and add the remaining ingredients except the chick pea flour and oil. Mix well and add the chick pea flour. Stir until the nuts are evenly coated.

Heat the oil in a wok or other suitable pan over a medium heat. When hot, but not smoking, add the nuts (in two batches if necessary) and fry them for 6–8 minutes or until they begin to crackle gently. Drain on kitchen paper. Allow to cool thoroughly before storing in an airtight jar. They will keep well for up to two weeks.

Great Indian Feasts

Sweet rice flakes with nuts

For me, this recipe takes me straight down memory lane! During Diwali, my mother would have a large sparkling silver bowl full of this delicious mix, displayed throughout the day so that anyone could help themselves, and no one could resist it! Rice flakes sold in supermarkets are much thinner and lighter than their Indian counterpart. The Indian ones have longer and more slender flakes and are creamy in colour. I love it for this recipe because it has more bite. However, I have tested the recipe with both varieties and am happy with the results. You need a large metal sieve and a wok or deep frying pan in which you can fry batches of rice flakes by lowering the sieve into the hot oil.

Serves 4–5

sunflower oil for deep-frying
25g/1oz raw cashew pieces
25g/1oz almonds, slivered
25g/1oz walnut halves, each
  broken up into 2–3 pieces
250g/9oz rice flakes
1–2 tablespoons caster sugar
½ teaspoon salt
½ teaspoon ground cumin
½ teaspoon freshly milled
  black pepper

Heat the oil over a medium heat. Using a sieve, fry the nuts, one variety at a time as they will need different cooking times. Cashews are ready when they are a medium-brown colour. Almonds will brown and crackle gently when they are ready. Walnuts are ready when they are light brown. Drain them on kitchen paper.

Increase the heat to high and allow the oil to heat until smoking point. Half fill a sieve with rice flakes and lower into the hot oil. They will puff up immediately and fill up the sieve. As soon as the sieve is full, drain the rice flakes on kitchen paper. When you have finished frying them all and while the rice flakes are still hot, add the fried nuts and sprinkle over the sugar, salt, cumin and pepper and mix thoroughly. When completely cooled, store in an airtight jar for up to six weeks.

Mridula Baljekar

Rose-scented mango cream

If you can get hold of Indian mango purée sold in cans in Asian stores, you will be totally hooked on this recipe, for Indian mangoes have a very distinctive taste and an unbeatable flavour. Otherwise, use sliced canned mangoes. As I love English summer fruits with a passion, I like to serve this dessert with fresh mixed berries such as blackberries, raspberries and blueberries. During the winter months, serve it scattered with pomegranate seeds.

Serves 6

50g/2oz granulated sugar
inner seeds of 6 cardamom
  pods
175ml/6fl oz evaporated milk
1 level tablespoon ground
  arrowroot
2 heaped tablespoons
  ground almonds
450g/1lb canned mango
  purée or 2 x 425g/15oz
  canned mangoes, drained
  and puréed
250g/9oz crème fraîche
2–3 drops rose essence or
  1 tablespoon rose water
summer fruits or toasted
  nuts, to decorate

Put the sugar and the cardamom seeds into a coffee or spice mill and grind until the seeds are a fine powder.

Put the evaporated milk into a heavy-based saucepan and place over a low heat. Add the cardamom-flavoured sugar, arrowroot blended with 4 tablespoons water and ground almond. Stir until the mixture has thickened.

Next, gradually add the mango purée beating the mixture with a wire whisk at the same time to ensure that no lumps are formed. Cook for a minute or two until the mixture has reached a thick custard consistency. Remove from the heat and allow to cool.

Stir the crème fraîche well and mix into the mango purée along with the rose essence or rose water. Chill the mixture for at least an hour then serve in stemmed glasses topped with fruits of your choice. You also can serve it on its own decorated with toasted nuts.

Golden chick pea flour rounds with cardamom and nutmeg

These are known as Besan (chick pea flour) Ladoo and although they easily qualify to be described as a sinful treat, they are pure pleasure! For me, Diwali would not be the same without them. They need constant attention during the first 12–15 minutes of cooking time, but, once you have tasted them, the effort put into making them will fade into insignificance!

Makes 28–30 balls

225g/8oz granulated sugar
inner seeds of 8 green
   cardamom pods
50g/2oz shelled raw
   pistachio nuts
225g/8oz ghee or unsalted
   butter
450g/1lb chick pea flour
   (besan), sieved
½ teaspoon freshly grated
   nutmeg

Transfer 4 tablespoons of the sugar into a coffee or spice mill and add the cardamom seeds. Grind it to a fine powder then mix with the remaining sugar and set aside.

Preheat a grill to high and toast the pistachio nuts until lightly browned, remove and cool.

In a heavy-based frying pan or other shallow pan, melt the ghee or butter over a low heat and add the sieved chick pea flour. Cook, stirring constantly, for 12–15 minutes until the flour is golden brown and releases the delicious toasted aroma.

Add the cardamom-flavoured sugar and nutmeg, mix thoroughly and remove from the heat.

Crush the toasted pistachio nuts lightly with a rolling pin and stir into the flour mixture.

Allow the mixture to cool completely and form into small walnut-sized balls. Store in an airtight container, where they will remain fresh for about four weeks.

Mridula Baljekar

Golden cubes in saffron-cream sauce

This is a bread pudding which is rich, delicious and totally guilt-ridden! Whenever I make it, I decide to ignore the guilt and enjoy its full glory. Traditionally, the bread is cut into cubes or triangles, but you can cut them into any shape you wish. The pudding is enriched with khoya which is made by boiling, then simmering full-fat milk, beyond the stage at which evaporated milk is produced. The milk solidifies to resemble the consistency of mashed potato. This is a process which requires plenty of time and patience! An easy alternative is to mix dried milk powder with single cream as I have suggested below. The pudding is garnished with edible silver leaves (varq), which is a Mogul tradition. Silver leaves are sold in Indian stores and they are not the easiest things to handle. I use silver dust, which you can buy from any shop where cake decorating ingredients are sold.

Serves 4

100g/3½oz dried milk powder
75ml/3fl oz single cream
4 large slices of day-or two-day-old white bread
sunflower or vegetable oil, for deep frying
300ml/10fl oz full cream milk
100g/3½oz caster sugar
1 tablespoon seedless raisins
a pinch of saffron threads, pounded
¼ teaspoon freshly grated nutmeg
1 tablespoon flaked almonds or pine kernels, toasted, and silver leaf or silver dust, to decorate (optional)

Mix the milk powder and cream together until well combined. Cover and chill for 1–2 hours.

Trim off the crusts from the bread and cut them into 2.5cm/1in cubes.

Heat the oil in a wok or other suitable pan over a medium heat. Fry the cubes of bread until they are well browned. Drain on kitchen paper.

In a separate pan, put the milk, sugar, raisins and saffron together and bring to simmering point. Add the fried bread and cook until the bread has absorbed all the milk.

Transfer the bread to a serving plate and sprinkle over the nutmeg, then spread the dried milk mixture over the top. If the mixture is hard, use a fork to break down any lumps first. Garnish with the almonds and silver leaf or silver dust, if using. Serve at room temperature.

Baked wheat squares

This is a fudge-like sweet known as a burfi, which is the generic name for sweets made this way using milk, cereals and nuts. Atta (chapatti flour) or a fine-textured wholemeal flour is ideal for this recipe. The total cooking time is approximately 15 minutes and you will need to give it your love and concentration for the whole time!

Serves 8–10

100g/3½ oz light soft brown sugar
inner seeds of 8 green cardamom pods
100g/3½oz ghee or unsalted butter
225g/8oz fine textured wholemeal flour
25g/1oz chopped mixed nuts

In a coffee or spice mill grind half the sugar and the cardamom seeds until fine then mix with the remaining sugar. Set aside.

Melt the ghee or butter over a medium heat and add the flour. Cook for 4–5 minutes, stirring constantly, then reduce the heat to low and continue to cook for a further 10–12 minutes or until the wonderful aroma of the toasted wheat is released. Stir constantly during this time.

Add the chopped nuts, cook for 1–2 minutes and remove from the heat then stir in the cardamom-flavoured sugar. If you see any lumps, break them down with the back of a wooden spoon.

Lightly grease a large plate or a baking sheet and spread the wheat mixture on it. Using the back of a metal spoon, spread the mixture evenly to form a rectangle approximately 15cm/6in x 20cm/8in x 1cm/½in. Let the mixture go cold, then chill for 15–20 minutes.

Remove from the fridge and cut into approximately 5cm/2in squares. Allow the burfi to harden before serving. Store in the fridge in an open container or on a plate. They will keep for 2–3 weeks.

Great Indian Feasts

Semolina and almond halva

Halva originated in the Middle East, where it is traditionally made with sesame seeds and sometimes almonds. North Indian cuisine has been influenced to a great extent by the ancient Persians and this version of halva, made with equal quantities of semolina, ground almond, clarified butter and sugar, is the ultimate comfort food! It is generally made without the almond as a religious offering to the elephant-headed Hindu god Ganesha, the remover of obstacles, and every ceremony begins with a special prayer to him. Once all the rituals are over and Ganesha has blessed the food, it is distributed to everyone.

Serves 6–8

1 tablespoon melted ghee
  or butter
25g/1oz raw cashews
1 tablespoon shelled raw
  pistachio nuts
125g/4oz semolina
125g/4oz ground almonds
125g/4oz ghee or unsalted
  butter
½ teaspoon ground nutmeg
½ teaspoon ground cardamom
125g/4oz caster sugar
300ml/½ pint full-cream milk

Brush a large plate with some melted ghee or butter and set aside. Preheat the grill to medium and toast the cashews and pistachio nuts, keeping them separate, until lightly browned. Cool and crush them lightly. Put them into separate bowls and set aside.

In a heavy-based pan, dry roast the semolina over a medium-low heat, stirring constantly for 6–8 minutes, until browned. Stir in the ground almonds, remove from the heat and set aside.

Melt the ghee or butter over a medium heat and add the nutmeg and cardamom. Follow quickly with the roasted semolina and almond mixture, sugar, milk and the pistachio nuts. Stir and cook until the mixture thickens and starts easing away from the bottom and sides of the pan.

Transfer the mixture to the greased plate and, using the back of a lightly greased metal spoon, spread it evenly to form a large square of about 1cm/½in thickness. Next, using a knife, press the sides inwards to form a neat, even square.

Sprinkle the toasted cashews evenly on top and press them lightly with the palm of your hand in order to secure them on the surface. Allow to cool, then cut into squares and serve. Store any leftovers in the fridge for up to a week. It is delicious both chilled and at room temperature.

Mridula Baljekar

Spiced dumplings in rose-scented cream sauce

This is a delicacy from the courts of the Mughal emperors where the practice of using floral essences was introduced to Indian cuisine. These little dumplings, with the enticing aroma of cardamom and nutmeg, smothered in a creamed fruit and nut sauce, are known as Shahi (Royal) Malpua. They are supremely delicious and rich. I have used a little orange rind in the sauce to balance the richness, which you can omit if you wish. If I make these at any other time, I like to add a little Cointreau in the sauce, which is not permitted during Diwali, as alcohol is taboo at this time!

Serves 6

25g/1oz ground rice
90g/3oz plain flour
50g/2oz caster sugar
small pinch of bicarbonate
   of soda
½ teaspoon ground cardamom
½ teaspoon freshly grated
   nutmeg
25g/1oz raw cashews, lightly
   crushed
125ml/4fl oz full-cream milk
sunflower oil, for deep frying
1 teaspoon ghee or unsalted
   butter
25g/1oz seedless raisins
1 tablespoon flaked almonds
300ml/½ pint single cream
finely grated rind of
   1 orange
3 dried, no-soak apricots,
   sliced
small pinch of saffron
   threads, pounded and
   infused in 1 tablespoon
   hot milk
1 tablespoon rose water

Put the ground rice, flour, caster sugar, bicarbonate of soda, cardamom, nutmeg and cashews into a bowl and mix well. Add the milk and stir until a thick batter is formed.

Heat the oil over a medium heat in a wok or other suitable pan for deep frying. Put in as many heaped teaspoons of the batter as the pan will hold in a single layer. Do not overcrowd the pan as this will lower the temperature which in turn will affect the consistency of the dumplings. When the dumplings start floating, turn them over, reduce the heat slightly and fry them until they are evenly browned. Drain on kitchen paper.

In a small pan, melt the ghee or butter and fry the raisins gently until they puff up. Remove with a slotted spoon. In the same fat, brown the flaked almonds and drain on kitchen paper.

In a pan large enough to hold all the dumplings, heat the cream, orange rind and sliced apricots together and bring to a slow simmer then let it cook for about a minute. Add the dumplings and turn them around gently. Reserve a few of the fried raisins and almonds and stir the remainder into the pan. Transfer the dumplings along with the sauce to a serving plate.

Mix the saffron milk and rose water together and sprinkle it over the dumplings. Garnish with the reserved raisins and almonds and serve.

Okra in roasted sesame and poppy seed sauce with coconut

Okra is known as Bhindi in India and is also referred to as ladies' fingers because of its shape. It is widely available in supermarkets. Many people do not use onion and garlic when cooking during religious festivals because they are believed to be stimulants, and one's mind should be void of all temptations during religious occasions! This is one of those recipes, but the absence of the two universally used ingredients in Indian cooking will hardly be missed, for it is delightful and highly addictive!

Serves 4

2 tablespoons sesame seeds
1 tablespoon white poppy
  seeds
2 dried red chillies, broken up
2 tablespoons desiccated
  coconut
275g/10oz okra
3 tablespoons sunflower or
  vegetable oil
½ teaspoon black mustard
  seeds
½ teaspoon cumin seeds
½ teaspoon salt

Heat a heavy-based saucepan or a griddle over a medium heat and dry-roast the sesame and poppy seeds, stirring constantly, until they are a shade darker (2–3 minutes). Transfer them to a plate and return the pan to heat. Add the chillies and coconut and roast, stirring constantly, until the coconut turns a light-brown colour (1–2 minutes). Transfer to another plate, keeping it separate from the seeds, and let it go cold.

Wash the okra, top and tail them and cut each one into 2–3 pieces depending on their size.

Heat the oil in a wok or other suitable pan over a medium heat. When hot, but not smoking, add the mustard seeds. As soon as they begin to pop, add the cumin and follow with the okra and salt. Stir-fry for 2–3 minutes, reduce the heat to low and cover the pan. Cook for 7–8 minutes.

Meanwhile, using a coffee or spice mill, grind the poppy and sesame seeds coarsely and add the chillies and coconut. Grind them until smooth. The oil in the seeds and the coconut will restrict the blade movement a little; simply stop the machine, scrape off everything from the blade and re-start.

Stir the ground ingredients into the okra and stir until the okra is fully coated with them. Remove from the heat and serve as a side dish.

Mridula Baljekar

Sweet puffed bread

These delicious little snacks are wicked! They are known as Mandhi and are one of the most popular sweets made during Diwali. They can be eaten on their own or as a dessert.

Makes 16

250g/9oz plain flour plus a
   little extra for dusting
200g/7oz semolina
150g/5oz granulated sugar
175ml/6fl oz water
50g/2oz ghee or unsalted
   butter
oil, for deep-frying

Combine the flour and semolina in a large mixing bowl.

Put the sugar and water into a saucepan and place over a medium heat. Stir until the sugar has dissolved then add the ghee or butter and stir until melted then add to the flour and semolina mixture.

Mix it thoroughly with a wooden spoon until a soft dough is formed. Cover with a damp cloth and let it cool.

When the dough is cold enough to handle, knead it until smooth and pliable. Divide the dough equally into two halves and make 8 portions from each half. Rotate between your palms and flatten into a cake. Dust each flattened cake in the extra flour and roll it out to a 7.5cm/3in-diameter circle.

Heat the oil, in a wok or other suitable pan for deep-frying, over a medium heat and fry the bread, one at a time, until they are well browned. Drain on kitchen paper.

COOK'S TIP
Traditionally, these sweet breads are eaten hot on their own, but I like to serve them when they have cooled slightly, accompanied by seasonal fruits and a scoop of vanilla ice cream.

Mridula Baljekar

Spice-coated crunchy potato slices

This is one of those Diwali delights which I enjoyed wholeheartedly during my childhood. This was a real favourite with all my brothers and sisters, and my mother used to make us do all sorts of household chores for an extra portion of these delicious morsels! I now serve these with drinks (not during Diwali!).

Serves 4–6

1 tablespoon ground rice
50g/2oz chick pea flour
  (besan)
½ teaspoon cumin seeds
½ teaspoon onion seeds
½ teaspoon fennel seeds
1–2 fresh red chillies, finely
  chopped (seeded, if liked)
½ teaspoon salt
450g/1lb potatoes, cut into
  5mm/¼in slices
sunflower or vegetable oil,
  for deep-frying

Mix all the ingredients up to and including the salt in a large bowl. Add 50ml/2fl oz cold water and mix until you have a thick paste. Next, add the potatoes and stir until they are fully coated with the paste.

Heat the oil in a wok or other suitable pan for deep-frying over a medium-high heat. Add as many batter-coated potato slices as the pan will hold in a single layer without overcrowding. Fry the slices until they are golden brown (7–8 minutes) and drain on kitchen paper. Serve immediately.

Cauliflower in spice-perfumed olive oil

Southern Indian in origin, this is known as Upkari, which is believed to have originated from two words belonging to a south-Indian language called Kannada. Upu means salt and kari means chilli, both of which are used in large quantities in the original recipe. Olive oil is a personal preference rather than a tradition. Again, note the absence of garlic and onion.

Serves 4

1 medium-sized cauliflower
2–3 tablespoons light olive oil
½ teaspoon black mustard seeds
½ teaspoon cumin seeds
5–6 fenugreek seeds
1–2 dried red chillies, scissor-snipped into small pieces
½ teaspoon salt
1 tablespoon desiccated coconut (optional)

Divide the cauliflower into 1cm/½in florets, wash and drain.

Heat the oil in a heavy-based pan over a medium heat. When hot, but not smoking, add the mustard seeds and, as soon as they begin to crackle, add the cumin seeds then the fenugreek and chillies.

Next, add the cauliflower and salt, reduce the heat to very low, cover the pan and sweat the cauliflower for 8–10 minutes until tender, but still firm.

Sprinkle the coconut over (if using), stir and remove from the heat.

Mridula Baljekar

Dried fruit and nut pilau

Growing up in the foothills of the Himalayas, I always enjoyed an exquisite variety of dried fruits and nuts brought down by handsome young Kashmiri traders. These are particularly in demand during Diwali. Here is an unusual pilau rice which can be eaten just with a raita or accompanied by grilled or roasted meat. If you have a nut allergy, simply omit them and replace with your choice of dried fruits.

Serves 4

225g/8oz basmati rice
4 tablespoons sunflower
  or vegetable oil
4 green cardamom pods,
  bruised
4 cloves
5cm/2in piece of cinnamon
  stick, halved
1 bay leaf
½ teaspoon back peppercorns
2 star anise
25g/1oz walnut pieces
25g/1oz blanched and
  slivered almonds
25g/1oz dried, ready-to-eat
  apricots, sliced
25g/1oz dried ready-to-eat
  plums, sliced
1 teaspoon salt
450ml/16fl oz lukewarm
  water
a good pinch of saffron
  threads, pounded and
  soaked in 2 tablespoons
  hot milk
1 tablespoon rose water
1 tablespoon pomegranate
  seeds, to garnish

Wash the rice in several changes of water by tossing and turning the grains gently until the water runs clear. Soak in cold water for 15–20 minutes and then drain in a colander.

In a heavy-based saucepan, heat the oil over a low heat and add the cardamom, cloves, cinnamon, bay leaf, peppercorns and star anise. Stir-fry them gently for 25–30 seconds and add the walnuts and almonds. Continue to fry for a further 30–40 seconds.

Add the drained rice, apricots, plums, salt and water. Stir once, bring it to the boil and cover the pan tightly. Reduce the heat to low and cook for 8–10 minutes, without lifting the lid.

Mix the saffron milk and the rose water together and sprinkle this randomly over the cooked rice and switch off the heat source. Cover the pan and leave it undisturbed for 8–10 minutes. Stir the rice gently with a flat metal or plastic spoon (wooden ones will squash the fragile grains) and transfer to a serving dish. Garnish with the pomegranate seeds for a spectacular appearance. You can eat the delicious seeds of the rest of the pomegranate!

Skinless split mung beans in fenugreek–coconut sauce

This is a very simple lentil dish with a clean and light taste. It is also nutritious as it offers protein, vitamins and minerals in one dish. The main flavours are fenugreek seeds and dried red chillies both of which are lightly fried and crushed and the perfumed oil is stirred into the lentils. Do take care when frying them because if you let them darken too much the fenugreek will lend a bitter taste. During Diwali this will be cooked without onion, but at any other time I add a finely chopped, medium-sized onion browned in a little oil right at the very end.

Mridula Baljekar

Serves 4

150g/5oz skinless split mung beans (mung dhal)

225g/8oz fresh spinach, chopped or frozen leaf spinach

125ml/4fl oz canned coconut milk

2 tablespoons sunflower or vegetable oil

2 dried red chillies, broken up

½ teaspoon fenugreek seeds

½ teaspoon ground turmeric

1 teaspoon salt

2 tablespoons lime juice

plain boiled basmati rice or Cardamom–scented Basmati Rice (page 135), to serve

Wash the lentils in several changes of water and soak in cold water for 1 hour. Drain and put into a saucepan with 600ml/1 pint water and bring it to the boil. Reduce the heat to medium–low and cook, uncovered, for 20–25 minutes.

Add the spinach and cook, uncovered, over a medium heat for 5–6 minutes or until the lentils and spinach have thickened. Add the coconut milk and simmer for a minute or two.

Next, heat the oil over a low heat and fry the chillies and fenugreek seeds until they are just a shade darker. Stir in the turmeric and remove from the heat. Let them cool then crush them in the oil with a pestle until you have a paste. Add this to the cooked lentils along with the salt. Stir in the lime juice and remove from the heat. Serve with plain boiled basmati rice or Cardamom-scented Basmati Rice.

VARIATION
Instead of spinach, you can use green beans or cauliflower florets.

Coconut-coated lentil and cucumber salad with mustard and lime

This salad is said to be a favourite of the Hindu god Rama in whose honour Diwali is celebrated. Rama returned in the evening after 14 years of exile and oil lamps were lit everywhere to welcome him back. This is why Diwali is also known as the Festival of Lights. Skinless split mung beans (known as mung dhal) are used for this salad and are sold by Indian grocers. If you cannot get them, use whole mung beans and add a few pieces of seeded and diced tomato for a contrast in colour.

Serves 4

50g/2oz skinless split mung beans (mung dhal)
1 medium–sized cucumber, finely diced
1 teaspoon English mustard
25g/1oz desiccated coconut
2 tablespoons lime juice
2 teaspoons sunflower or vegetable oil
½ teaspoon black mustard seeds
1–2 dried red chillies, scissor-snipped into small pieces
½ teaspoon cumin seeds
½ teaspoon salt

Wash the mung beans in several changes of water and soak in cold water for 3–4 hours. You could soak it overnight if you wish. Drain thoroughly.

Put the cucumber in a mixing bowl and add the drained mung beans and the mustard. Mix well.

Grind the coconut in a coffee or spice mill or use a mortar and pestle (this improves its texture and taste) and add to the cucumber mix. Add the lime juice and mix thoroughly.

In a small saucepan or a ladle, heat the oil over a medium heat. When hot, but not smoking, add the mustard seeds. As soon as they crackle add the chillies, let them blacken then add the cumin seeds, and switch off the heat source. Pour the mixture over the salad and stir thoroughly. Stir in the salt just before serving.

Cardamom-scented basmati rice

Cardamom is known as the queen in the kingdom of spices. Next to saffron, it is the most expensive spice in the world. Cardamom seeds are prized for their sweet, lingering aroma. In India, the seeds are chewed as a breath freshener. Always choose the plump green cardamom pods with tightly closed skins. Once the skin splits, the volatile oil dries up fast and the flavour diminishes quickly. This is not particularly a Diwali speciality, but is a perfect alternative to pilau rice when time is short. It also complements most curries.

Serves 4–6

275g/10oz basmati rice
15g/½oz unsalted butter
2 tablespoons sunflower or
    olive oil
8 green cardamom pods,
    bruised
2 bay leaves
1 teaspoon salt or to taste
500ml/18fl oz hand-hot water

Wash the rice in several changes of water until it runs clear. Soak it in cold water for 15–20 minutes then drain in a colander.

In a heavy-based saucepan, heat the butter and oil together over a low heat. Add the cardamom pods and the bay leaves and let them sizzle for 25–30 seconds.

Add the drained rice and salt, stir gently and pour in the hot water. Raise the heat and bring it to the boil and let it boil steadily for about a minute. Reduce the heat to low, cover the pan tightly and cook for 8–10 minutes. Switch off the heat source and let it stand, undisturbed, for 6–8 minutes. Fluff up the rice with a fork and transfer to a serving dish.

Mridula Baljekar

Carrot raita seasoned with mustard and cumin-scented hot oil

This is a quick, easy and highly nutritious side dish for all occasions and it will easily fit into any religious Indian festival menu because of the absence of onion and garlic. The hot oil seasoning with the black mustard seeds adds a deliciously nutty taste and the cumin adds warmth and slight pungency without being harsh.

Serves 4

225g/8oz carrots, diced
25g/1oz desiccated coconut
1 green chilli, chopped
  (seeded, if wished)
150g/5oz whole milk plain
  yogurt
½ teaspoon salt
1 tablespoon sunflower or
  vegetable oil
½ teaspoon black mustard
  seeds
½ teaspoon cumin seeds

Steam the carrots until al dente and leave to cool.

Grind the coconut and the green chilli in a coffee or spice mill.

Beat the yogurt until smooth and add the salt, carrots and coconut and chilli mixture.

In a small pan, wok or a ladle, heat the oil over a medium heat. When hot, but not smoking, add the mustard seeds. When they begin to pop, add the cumin and switch off the heat source. Pour the flavoured oil over the raita, stir to mix well and serve.

Sesame rice

Sesame rice is delicious with all sorts of Indian dishes. You can use a mortar and pestle to grind the sesame seeds and the dried red chillies together. If you cut the chillies into small pieces (easier with a pair of scissors), it will make the grinding easier whether you use mortar and pestle or a coffee mill. The mixture does not need to be super fine.

Serves 4

225g/8oz basmati rice, washed and soaked for 15 minutes
½ teaspoon salt or to taste
2 tablespoons sesame seeds
2–4 dried red chillies, cut into small pieces
2 tablespoons sunflower or vegetable oil
½ teaspoon black mustard seeds
½ teaspoon cumin seeds
½ teaspoon ground turmeric

Drain the rice thoroughly and place in a saucepan. Add the salt and pour in 475ml/16 fl oz hot water. Bring to the boil, and allow to boil steadily for 1-2 minutes. Reduce the heat to low, cover the pan and cook for 8 minutes without lifting the lid. Remove from the heat and leave it undisturbed for 6-7 minutes, then fork through and set aside.

Meanwhile, grind the sesame seeds and the chillies together.

Heat the oil over a medium heat in a large saucepan or a sauté pan, preferably with a non-stick surface. When hot, but not smoking, throw in the mustard seeds, followed by the cumin.

Stir in the turmeric and follow quickly with the ground sesame/chilli mixture. Cook for 1 minute, then carefully fold in the cooked rice.

Mridula Baljekar

Christmas

Christmas is a special time, and the weeks leading up to it are exciting, although exhausting. Traditional British Christmas feasts are fabulous, and their origins fascinating. Although I am not a Christian, I have lived in Britain long enough to feel part of these festivities. My two daughters, having been born and brought up here, have always enjoyed traditional Christmas food. I have taken as much care in making my own Christmas cakes and puddings, as I have in preparing sweets during Diwali, the Hindu Festival of Lights.

Over the years I have written several recipes for an alternative Christmas for magazines and newspapers here in Britain as well as in India and Australia. As Britain is emerging as a melting pot of diverse and traditional cuisine and culture, I feel it will be a fitting tribute to offer a chapter with recipes which can be used at Christmas time as well as for other celebrations.

Indian food is very popular in Britain today. Although it is generally perceived to be difficult and time-consuming to make, once you have bought your spices and stored them correctly, you are ready to turn out superb meals any time you want. All you need to buy are the fresh ingredients, which can be easily fitted into your weekly shopping plan. With all the stress of Christmas shopping and other associated traditions to follow, at least you won't have to get up early on Christmas morning to make sure that you are working to a strict timetable to put the turkey in the oven, take it out in time to be able to use the oven for the accompaniments, and then make sure that everything comes out of the oven and goes to the dining table at precisely the right time! You can cook your alternative Indian-style Christmas lunch up to 48 hours ahead of time with only a few last-minute preparations to do on the day, enabling you to indulge in a more relaxed and enjoyable Christmas lunch.

Celebration recipes from India take centre stage in this book. Although this is a special section on traditional Christmas produce with an Indian twist, any of the other festive recipes are ideal on Christmas Day. From fabulous finger foods and canapés, to intriguing main courses, to desserts with contemporary influences, I am sure you will delight your family and friends on Christmas Day. The essence of this whole idea is for you to keep calm and relaxed and turn out a fantastic feast at the same time! Most importantly, once you have all the food on the table, you can sit and enjoy your meal with everyone else, without having to get up!

Mridula Baljekar

Choosing the right wine

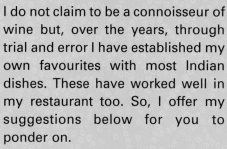

I do not claim to be a connoisseur of wine but, over the years, through trial and error I have established my own favourites with most Indian dishes. These have worked well in my restaurant too. So, I offer my suggestions below for you to ponder on.

The special ones in the Christmas Drinks (page 153) section are ideal with the canapés and first courses, but if you prefer just wine then choose easy-drinking whites which are fresh and light such as Pinot Grigio or Pinot Blanc. Soft and fruity rosés such as Grenache work well. Low-tannin reds are good too; my favourites are Merlot and Rioja. Of course, given a choice, I would drink Champagne all the way!

To go with the rich and creamy main course dishes, I like whites with an assertive flavour and more body such as a Chardonnay, Sauvignon Blanc and Australian or New Zealand Riesling. Riesling tends to cut the sharpness in food, while the crisp nature of Sauvignon Blanc complements tikkas and other kebabs. Certain rosé wines which also have an assertive nature can take the weight of the spices.

Spanish rosé from Navarra and French rosé from Côtes de Provence have coped well. If you would rather have red, then my suggestion would be those which are really rich and generous in nature such as Cabernet Sauvignon, Malbec and Pinot Noir.

Fiery dishes are best accompanied by really well-chilled, very rich whites. Look at the range from the Loire Valley or try a Gewurztraminer from Alsace Among the reds, I prefer to stay with low-tannin wines such as Sangiovese, Merlot, Gamay and young Rioja.

Drinking lager with Indian food is a British tradition which has long been established. It is a matter of individual preference, although I lean more towards wine. Many people still have a misconception that wine does not complement Indian food. We have come a long way from those days as fabulous wines are now being produced to complement spicy food.

In India, drinking wine with food is still a very new concept. In fact, alcohol is rarely consumed with food as most of the drinking is done before dinner. Plain water is what everyone prefers.

Oven-roasted pecan nuts with chilli and cumin

This recipe is an adaptation of a deliciously spiced version I had in Texas, the home of pecan nuts. It had a kind of sweet and savoury taste, with a mildly intoxicating kick because of the pasilla chilli powder they used. You can make these nuts up to a week in advance.

Serves 10–12

450g/1lb pecan halves
6 tablespoons melted
   unsalted butter
1 teaspoon ground cumin
1 teaspoon hot chilli powder
½ teaspoon garlic powder
1 teaspoon soft brown sugar
½ teaspoon salt

Preheat the oven to 180°C/350°F/Gas Mark 4.

Mix the pecan halves and the melted butter until the nuts are fully coated. Sprinkle the remaining ingredients over and mix thoroughly. Place the nuts in a shallow ovenproof dish. Be sure to scrape off any remaining residue of the spice mix and blend it with the nuts, arranging them in a single layer. Bake them in the centre of the oven for 10–12 minutes or until the nuts are browned. Remove them from the oven and allow to cool, then store in an airtight jar. They will keep well for 4–5 weeks.

Mridula Baljekar

Spiced chick pea-filled croustades

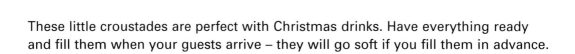

These little croustades are perfect with Christmas drinks. Have everything ready and fill them when your guests arrive – they will go soft if you fill them in advance. They can be bought from good supermarkets.

Makes 24

400g/14oz can chick peas
2 tablespoons finely chopped
    spring onions
1–2 green chillies, finely
    chopped
2 tablespoons finely chopped
    fresh coriander leaves
1 tablespoon lemon juice
salt, to taste
1 packet of 24 mini
    croustades
2 tablespoons plain yogurt,
    beaten
½ teaspoon mint chutney
¼ teaspoon sugar
2 teaspoons chilli sauce

Drain the chick peas and rinse them well. Put them in a bowl and add the spring onions, chillies, coriander, lemon juice and salt to taste.

Divide the chick pea mixture among the 24 croustades.

Beat the yogurt until smooth and add the mint chutney, salt and sugar. Divide the yogurt mixture equally among the 24 filled croustades. Top with the chilli sauce and serve.

Herbed sweet potato croquettes

These are yummy with Christmas drinks. You can make these on Christmas Eve, then refrigerate and fry them on Christmas Day. They will also hold their shape better once chilled. Serve them on their own or with Rhubarb and Raisin Chutney (page 179).

Makes 20

550g/1¼lb sweet potatoes,
  finely grated
2–3 shallots, finely chopped
1–3 green chillies, finely
  chopped, seeded, if wished
1 tablespoon finely chopped
  fresh coriander leaves
1 tablespoon finely chopped
  fresh thyme
1 tablespoon snipped fresh
  chives
1 teaspoons salt
½ teaspoon aniseed
½ teaspoon onion seeds
1 teaspoon cumin seeds
125g/4oz chick pea flour
  (besan)
50g/2oz cornmeal
4–5 tablespoons water
sunflower oil, for deep-frying

Put the grated sweet potato in a large mixing bowl and add the remaining ingredients except the water and oil. Mix thoroughly with your fingertips to bind the ingredients together. Add 1 tablespoon water at a time until you have a moist, but not wet, mixture. You may not need all of the water. Make 20 walnut-sized balls and shape them into croquettes.

Heat the oil over a medium-high heat in a wok or other suitable pan for deep-frying. Fry the croquettes in batches until they are golden brown and drain on kitchen paper.

Great Indian Feasts

Mini venison kebabs with melted chilli-cheese

These delicious little kebabs are very moreish. They go down really well with a glass of full-bodied red wine.

Makes 20–24

50g/2oz natural cashew pieces
1 large egg
2 tablespoons single cream
1 slice white bread, crusts removed and cut into small pieces
1 small red onion, roughly chopped
2 large garlic cloves, roughly chopped
2.5cm/1in piece root ginger, roughly chopped
1–3 green chillies, roughly chopped (seeded, if wished)
2–3 tablespoons roughly chopped fresh coriander leaves
1 tablespoon finely chopped fresh mint leaves
1 teaspoon garam masala
½ teaspoon salt or to taste
450g/1lb lean minced venison
olive oil, for brushing

FOR THE TOPPING
50g/2oz Cheddar cheese, grated
1–2 Thai red chillies, finely chopped
1 tablespoon snipped fresh chives

Process the cashews, egg, cream and bread until smooth. Add the remaining ingredients, except the oil and process until fine. Chill the mixture for 30–40 minutes or leave overnight.

Preheat the grill to high. Line a grill pan with foil and brush with a little oil.

Next, divide the mixture into 20–24 equal-sized portions and flatten into mini cakes. Place them on the prepared grill pan and brush them over with oil. Grill approximately 7.5cm/3in below the heat source for 2–3 minutes. Turn them over and brush the uncooked side with oil. Grill for a further 2–3 minutes.

Mix together the ingredients for the topping. Move the cooked kebabs close together without leaving any gaps. Sprinkle the cheese mixture evenly on top and place under the grill until the cheese has melted. Carefully separate the kebabs with a knife or a fish slice and transfer them to a serving plate.

Mridula Baljekar

Prawn and smoked haddock koftas

These koftas are quick and easy to make. You can use just prawns, although I find haddock adds an exotic touch and a superb taste sensation.

Makes 18

1 large egg
2 large slices of white bread, crusts removed
1–2 green chillies, (seeded, if wished)
2.5cm/1in piece root ginger, roughly chopped
2 garlic cloves, roughly chopped
200g/7oz cooked and peeled small prawns (thawed and drained if frozen)
200g/7oz smoked haddock, roughly chopped
2–3 tablespoons finely chopped fresh coriander leaves
6–8 fresh mint leaves, finely chopped
2–3 shallots, finely chopped
½ teaspoon fennel seeds, crushed
¼ teaspoon salt
sunflower oil, for deep-frying

Put the egg, bread, chillies, ginger and garlic in a food processor and blend until smooth.

Add the prawns and haddock and, using the pulse action, blend them to a coarse mixture, then transfer to a mixing bowl. Add the remaining ingredients except the salt. Mix well and form the mixture into 18 walnut-sized balls.

Heat the oil in a wok or other suitable pan over medium-high heat and fry the koftas in batches until golden brown. Drain on kitchen paper. Serve with a mango dip (see Cook's Tip).

COOK'S TIP
Make a simple mango dip by blending together 90g/3oz mango chutney and 90g/3oz crème fraîche. Add salt to taste and a little hot chilli powder if you like. Chill the dip before serving.

Coriander-crusted chicken with mango

Chicken and mango is definitely a winning combination! Here, the sweet and mellow ground coriander complements the tartness of the mango beautifully. Make sure you add the mango when the chicken is cold otherwise the fruit will lose its character.

Serves 8–10

1 tablespoon ground
  coriander seeds
450g/1lb boned chicken
  breasts, skin removed
3 tablespoons sunflower
  or olive oil
4–6 large garlic cloves,
  crushed
½ teaspoon chilli powder
½ teaspoon salt
3 tablespoons lime juice
3 tablespoons finely chopped
  fresh coriander
1 large ripe fresh mango,
  cut into 1cm/½in cubes

Using a coffee grinder or mortar and pestle, grind the coriander seeds to a coarse texture.

Cut the chicken into 1cm/½in cubes.

Heat the oil in a large, non-stick frying pan over a low heat. When hot, add the garlic and fry until it is lightly browned.

Increase the heat to medium-high and add the chicken, then stir-fry for 8–10 minutes.

Add the ground coriander and chilli powder and continue to stir-fry for 3–4 minutes, stirring constantly. Add the lime juice and stir-fry for about a minute. Stir in the coriander leaves, remove from the heat and let cool.

Arrange a piece of chicken and a cube of mango on cocktail sticks and serve.

VARIATION
For a vegetarian version, use cubed mango, pineapple and feta cheese. Cook the spices as above, take the pan off the heat and toss in the fruits and cheese.

Mridula Baljekar

Turkey and guinea fowl kebabs

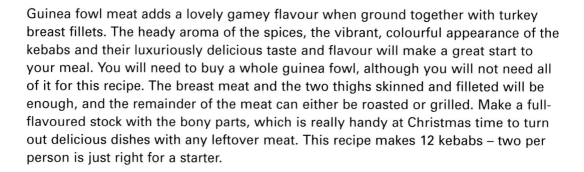

Guinea fowl meat adds a lovely gamey flavour when ground together with turkey breast fillets. The heady aroma of the spices, the vibrant, colourful appearance of the kebabs and their luxuriously delicious taste and flavour will make a great start to your meal. You will need to buy a whole guinea fowl, although you will not need all of it for this recipe. The breast meat and the two thighs skinned and filleted will be enough, and the remainder of the meat can either be roasted or grilled. Make a full-flavoured stock with the bony parts, which is really handy at Christmas time to turn out delicious dishes with any leftover meat. This recipe makes 12 kebabs – two per person is just right for a starter.

Makes 12

50g/2oz raw cashews
1 large egg
50g/2oz mild Cheddar cheese, cut into small chunks
2.5cm/1in piece root ginger, roughly chopped
3 large garlic cloves, roughly chopped
350g/12oz turkey breast fillets, roughly chopped
350g/12oz guinea fowl, roughly chopped
1 onion, roughly chopped
1 teaspoon salt
1 tablespoon ground coriander
1 teaspoon garam masala
2 fresh red chillies, finely chopped
1 tablespoon chopped fresh mint leaves
15g/½oz coriander leaves and stalks, chopped
50g/2oz butter melted

Preheat the grill to high and line a grill pan with foil, then brush with some oil.

In a food processor blend together the cashews, egg, cheese, ginger and garlic. Add the meat, onion, salt and the spices. Blend until everything is well incorporated.

Transfer the mixture to a large mixing bowl and add the chillies, mint and coriander. Don't be tempted to put these ingredients in the processor. Using them this way creates a spectacular appearance for the kebabs.

Divide the mixture into 12 equal-sized portions and form each into a sausage shape. Arrange the kebabs on the prepared grill pan and brush them generously with some of the melted butter. Grill approximately 13cm/5in below the heat source for 5–6 minutes. Turn them over, brush with the remaining melted butter and grill for 3–4 minutes. Remove and serve immediately with Spiced Cranberry Chutney (page 177).

Stuffed crabs

The influence of European culture on Goa's heritage is reflected in its cuisine. This recipe is a perfect blend of East and West.

Serves 4

4 cooked crabs weighing about 450g/1lb each
3 tablespoons oil
1 small onion, finely chopped
2 green chillies, finely chopped
2 teaspoons freshly grated or puréed ginger
2 teaspoons crushed or puréed garlic
1 teaspoon ground coriander
½ teaspoon ground fennel
50g/2oz sweet red pepper, finely chopped
salt to taste
1 fresh tomato, seeded and finely chopped
2 tablespoons lime juice
50g/2oz butter
1 teaspoon finely chopped garlic
25g/1oz fresh breadcrumbs
2 tablespoons chopped fresh dill leaves
shredded lettuce, to serve

Lay the cooked crab on its back and break off the claws and legs with a twisting action. Tap the claws and legs gently with a rolling pin to crack them without breaking into lots of small pieces. Extract the meat and discard the shells.

Pull the centre portion from the main shell. Extract the meat with a teaspoon. Use a skewer for the stubborn bits. Discard the thick dark-brown bits. Discard the stomach sac, gills and lungs. Wash the shells and wipe dry with absorbent kitchen paper. Brush lightly with oil.

Heat the oil over a medium heat and fry the onion, green chillies and ginger until the onions are soft but not brown.

Add the coriander, fennel, pepper and salt. Cook for 1 minute and add the tomato. Cook for a further minute.

Add the crabmeat and lime juice, mix well and cook gently until the crabmeat is heated through. Remove from the heat and keep hot.

Heat the butter gently and fry the garlic until light brown, then add the breadcrumbs. Stir until the breadcrumbs are browned, stir in the dill and remove.

Put the spiced crabmeat into the shells. Top with the spiced breadcrumbs and serve on a bed of shredded lettuce.

Mridula Baljekar

Vermicelli-coated spinach patties

As well as serving as a starter, these fabulously flavoured vegetable and mozzarella patties can be served as part of a buffet lunch or dinner. The patties are fried until the vermicelli coating transforms into a pale golden colour and the emerald green spinach shows through the strands of vermicelli to create a stunning appearance.

Makes 12

375g/13oz frozen leaf spinach
90g/3oz boiled potatoes, mashed
90g/3oz mozzarella cheese, grated
2.5cm/1in piece root ginger, finely grated
2 large garlic cloves, crushed to a fine pulp
1 teaspoon fennel seeds, crushed
½ teaspoon garam masala
1 fresh red chilli, finely chopped (seeded, if wished)
¾ teaspoon salt
90g/3oz plain vermicelli
1½ tablespoons cornflour
1 medium egg, beaten
light olive oil, for deep-frying
Apricot Chutney (page 178), to serve

Thaw the spinach and squeeze out all the liquid then chop finely. Put into a mixing bowl and add the potatoes, mozzarella, ginger and garlic. Mix thoroughly and add the fennel, garam masala, chilli and salt. Blend well.

Divide the mixture into two equal portions and make 6 smaller portions out of each. Form them into flat cakes of about 1cm/½in thickness, cover with clingfilm and refrigerate for 30 minutes.

Break up the cluster of vermicelli into smaller pieces about 2.5cm/1in long and put them into a bowl.

Dust each cake in the cornflour, making sure they are fully coated. Dip them into the beaten egg and roll in the vermicelli. The patties should be coated with the vermicelli quite generously to resemble a miniature nest.

Heat the oil over a medium heat in a wok or other suitable pan for deep-frying. Fry the patties in batches without overcrowding the pan until they are golden brown on both sides. Drain on kitchen paper and serve hot with Apricot Chutney.

Spiced avocado pâté with chilli-garlic prawns

Another Western dish with an Indian twist, which not only exudes an aura of luxury but is also a sheer delight to the palate.

Serves 4–5

FOR THE PÂTÉ
2 ripe avocados
finely grated zest and juice
  of 1 lemon
2 small green chillies,
  chopped
2–3 tablespoons coriander
  leaves, chopped
1 small garlic clove, crushed
75g/3oz cream cheese
½ teaspoon roasted ground
  cumin
salt and freshly milled black
  pepper

FOR THE PRAWNS
2 tablespoons light olive oil
2–3 shallots, finely chopped
4 garlic cloves, finely
  chopped
1–2 fresh red chillies,
  preferably Thai, finely
  chopped
250g/9oz cooked and peeled
  small prawns, thawed and
  drained if frozen
2 tablespoons finely chopped
  fresh coriander leaves
naan or pitta bread, to serve

Peel and stone the avocados and chop them roughly. Put them in a blender with the lemon zest and juice, chillies, coriander leaves, garlic and cream cheese and roasted cumin then blend until smooth. Season to taste and refrigerate for 2–3 hours.

Meanwhile, heat the oil over a low heat and gently sauté the shallots, garlic and chillies until the shallots are just beginning to colour. Remove from the heat and fold in the prawns and the coriander leaves.

Set the pâté into individual ring moulds on serving plates and divide the prawns equally among them. Remove the ring moulds and serve with strips of warm naan or pitta bread.

VARIATION
For a vegetarian alternative use 250g/9oz diced mango instead of the prawns.

Mridula Baljekar

Smoked salmon on parsnip and sweet potato cake

The earthy, wholesome taste of the root vegetables are intensified with a touch of spice. Chopped smoked salmon tossed in lime juice, chilli and coriander served on the vegetable cakes will surely enliven your taste buds. You can use any other smoked fish such as mackerel or haddock if you prefer.

Makes 8

200–225g/7–8oz smoked
  salmon
1½ tablespoons lime juice
1–2 green chillies, seeded
  and finely chopped
1 shallot, finely chopped
1 tablespoon finely chopped
  fresh coriander leaves

FOR THE CAKES
175g/6oz parsnips, grated
275g/10oz sweet potato,
  grated
1 small onion, finely chopped
15g/½oz coriander leaves
  and stalks, finely chopped
½–1 teaspoon chilli powder
1 teaspoon salt
1 teaspoon onion seeds
1 teaspoon aniseed
90g/3oz cornmeal
90g/3oz cornflour
150ml/5fl oz water
oil, for shallow-frying
crème fraîche, rocket leaves
  and fresh dill, to serve
Pineapple Chutney, to serve
  (page 180)

Flake the fish and put into a mixing bowl. Add the remaining ingredients, toss them around gently and set aside.

Meanwhile, in a large mixing bowl, mix all the ingredients for the spiced cakes, except the oil. Shape the mixture into eight 1cm/½in-thick cakes. If they feel slightly crumbly, do not worry, once they are in the hot oil, they will set quickly.

Pour enough oil in a frying pan to cover the base to a depth of approximately 2.5cm/1in. Heat over a medium heat and fry the vegetable cakes in batches, without overcrowding the pan. Do not turn them over until you have fried one side for at least 3 minutes. Drain on absorbent paper when browned on both sides.

Pile the spiced salmon on the vegetable cakes and spoon a little crème fraîche on top. Arrange the rocket leaves in the centre of a serving plate and place the prepared cakes on them. Garnish with dill sprigs.

VARIATION
The spiced cakes are delicious without the salmon topping. As a vegetarian alternative, serve them with a topping of Pineapple Chutney.

Spinach and potato soup with an aromatic bouillon (caldo verde)

Goa, known as the Pearl of the East, has a rich culinary heritage influenced by the Portuguese when they colonised this part of India in the 16th century. This soup is a classic example of the Indo-Portuguese style of cooking that is prevalent in Goa even today. A good, aromatic stock (bouillon) is essential to produce an exquisitely delicious soup. The recipe below makes a fabulous stock which you can freeze and use for other soups and stews.

Serves 5–6

FOR THE AROMATIC BOUILLON

250g/9oz cooked chicken
   carcass, cut up
250g/9oz raw beef bones
250g/9oz raw lamb bones
2 large onions, unpeeled
   and quartered
6 large garlic cloves,
   unpeeled and bruised
2.5cm/1in piece root ginger,
   unpeeled and sliced
1 teaspoon black peppercorns
2 x 2.5cm/1in pieces of
   cinnamon sticks
3 star anise
4 cloves
2 carrots, thickly sliced
1 stick celery, chopped

FOR THE SOUP

1 tablespoon butter
1 tablespoon olive oil
1 medium onion, chopped
2–3 garlic cloves, minced
600ml/1 pint aromatic bouillon
1 large potato, chopped
125g/4oz fresh spinach
   leaves, chopped
150ml/5fl oz single cream
crème fraîche

To make the stock, put all the ingredients, except the seasoning, into a large pan and add 2.5 litres/4 pints water. Bring it to the boil, skim off any scum from the surface, cover the pan and simmer for 45–50 minutes. Leave the saucepan in a cool place and, when the contents are completely cold, place it in the refrigerator for 2–3 hours. After this time, the fat will solidify. Remove all the fat with a perforated spoon and strain the stock. Season the stock with salt and freshly milled pepper.

To make the soup, heat the butter and oil together over a medium heat and fry the onion and garlic until they begin to brown.

Add the stock, potatoes, spinach and salt to season. Bring it to the boil, cover the pan and simmer for 10–15 minutes or until the potatoes are tender.

Remove from the heat, cool slightly and purée the soup. Return it to a clean pan, season with pepper and add the cream. Heat gently without boiling and serve swirled with the crème fraîche.

VARIATION

For a vegetarian option, replace all the meat bones with equal quantities of chopped celery, carrots and cabbage.

Pineapple punch

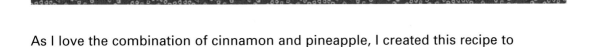

As I love the combination of cinnamon and pineapple, I created this recipe to welcome my Christmas guests. I often serve it instead of mulled wine and everyone seems to like it! I think it is best served warm.

Serves 8–10

500ml/18fl oz water
2 x 2.5cm/1in pieces of cinnamon stick
8 cloves
8 green cardamom pods, bruised
2–3 tablespoons chopped fresh mint leaves
1.1 litres/2 pints sweetened pineapple juice
200ml/7fl oz brandy
3 tablespoons Cointreau
caster sugar, to taste

Put the water, cinnamon, cloves and cardamom into a saucepan and bring to the boil. Reduce the heat to low and simmer for 10–12 minutes. Remove from the heat and allow to cool, then strain through a fine sieve.

Mix the spiced liquid with the pineapple juice, brandy and Cointreau. Taste it and add a little caster sugar if needed.

153

Mridula Baljekar

Mango bellini

You need mango purée for this drink, which you can easily make at home. Although fresh mango purée is ideal, I often make it with canned mango purée, especially at Christmas time when we all feel we need to add a few extra hours to our day! If you want to make fresh mango purée, add the juice of a lime and sugar to taste.

Serves 6

150ml/5fl oz mango purée
1 bottle chilled Champagne
6 slices of ripe mango

Simply divide the mango purée among 6 Champagne flutes and top with chilled Champagne. Garnish with a mango slice and serve.

Mridula Baljekar

Mango and melon fizz

This is a sure-fire success with teetotallers! You need really ripe fruits for this drink, so buy them a few days in advance and leave at room temperature to ripen. The mango should give a little when pressed gently with your fingertip. Ginger gives this drink a real boost; I like to use both ginger ale and a little fresh ginger, but you can omit the latter if you wish.

Serves 6

1 large, ripe mango
½ ripe galia melon
850ml/1½ pints ginger ale
½ teaspoon grated root ginger
crushed ice and sprigs of fresh mint, to serve

Peel the mango and slice off from either side of the stone, then slice off the two smaller sides. Chop them roughly.

Peel, seed and chop the melon and put it in a blender with the mango, add half the ginger ale and the root ginger. Purée until the ingredients are smooth then blend in the remaining ginger ale.

Line tall glasses with crushed ice and pour in the drink. Serve garnished with sprigs of mint.

Great Indian Feasts

Lychee and pomegranate crush

Pomegranates have become a regular feature on the supermarket shelves and they reach their peak during the winter months. Choose ones with a rich red skin because only they will have the vibrant, burgundy-coloured juicy seeds inside. Buy fresh lychees if you can, though canned ones can be used.

Serves 4

4–5 ripe pomegranates
10 fresh lychees
crushed ice and sprigs of
   fresh mint, to serve

Halve each pomegranate and peel off the skin like an orange. If it is difficult to peel, hold the pomegranate half with one hand, the cut side down and tap the skin gently all around with the handle of a large knife. Peel the fruit over a bowl so that you can collect every bit of the richly coloured, delicious juice.

Once you have removed the outer skin, you will also need to peel off the white pith and membrane which hold the seeds together. They do come off quite easily. The seeds are sweet with a slightly sour undertone and have a delicate bouquet which makes it difficult not to pop them in your mouth as you go along!

Peel the lychees like you would peel an orange and, once peeled, slit it in the middle or top of each fruit then ease away the flesh from the stone.

Reserve a few pomegranate seeds and put the remainder in a blender along with the lychees. Blend until smooth, then strain the juice. Push the pulp through with a spoon to extract as much juice as possible. Line tall glasses with crushed ice and pour in the juice. Place the reserved seeds on top and garnish with a sprig of mint.

Mridula Baljekar

Cranberry lassi

This is a deliberate attempt to make a large quantity of this drink for it not only adds a festive touch with cranberries, but will also rescue you from the after-effects of Christmas bingeing as yogurt is known to cure hangovers!

Makes 1.5 litres/2½ pints

1.1 litres/2 pints cranberry juice
450g/1lb whole milk plain yogurt
caster sugar, to taste
crushed ice and ground cinnamon, to serve

Mix everything together in a blender and chill. Serve topped with crushed ice sprinkled with ground cinnamon.

Venison steaks in chilli-tomato sauce

This recipe, with cubed venison steaks wrapped in a fragrant tomato sauce, offers you ravishing flavours. It should also delight the diet-conscious as venison is virtually fat-free.

159

Mridula Baljekar

Serves 4

750g/1½lb venison leg steaks, cut into 2.5cm/1in cubes
90g/3oz whole milk plain yogurt, beaten until smooth
2 tablespoons red wine vinegar
½ teaspoon ground turmeric
1 tablespoon ginger purée
1 tablespoon garlic purée
1 teaspoon salt
4 tablespoons sunflower or olive oil
½ teaspoon fennel seeds
½ teaspoon onion seeds
1 large onion, very finely chopped
1½ teaspoons ground cumin
½ teaspoon ground fennel
½ –2 teaspoons chilli powder
2 ripe salad tomatoes, skinned and chopped
½ teaspoon sugar
1 tablespoon tomato purée
1 teaspoon garam masala
2–3 tablespoons chopped fresh coriander
basmati rice or Garlic and Rosemary Naan with Truffle Oil (page 172)

Put the meat into a non-metallic bowl. Mix together the beaten yogurt, vinegar, turmeric, ginger, garlic and salt then pour over the meat. Stir until the meat is thoroughly coated. Cover and refrigerate for at least 4 hours or overnight. Bring it to room temperature before cooking.

Transfer the marinated meat to a heavy-based saucepan and add 150ml/¼ pint water, then bring it to a simmering point over a low heat. Cover and cook for 45–50 minutes, stirring occasionally. Remove the meat with a slotted spoon and strain the stock into a measuring jug. Make it up to 450ml/16fl oz with water and set aside.

Heat the oil over a medium heat and add the fennel and onion seeds and allow them to sizzle for 15–20 seconds. Add the onion and stir-fry until it just begins to brown then add the cooked meat and stir-fry for 4–5 minutes, reducing the heat slightly towards the end.

Add the cumin, fennel, chilli powder and tomatoes. Stir-fry for 3–4 minutes, then add 50ml/2fl oz water and continue to stir-fry for 2–3 minutes. Add the reserved stock, sugar and tomato purée. Bring it to the boil, reduce the heat and simmer, uncovered, for 10–12 minutes. Add the garam masala and simmer for 30–40 seconds, stir in the coriander leaves and remove from the heat. Serve with steamed basmati rice or Garlic and Rosemary Naan with Truffle Oil.

Cauliflower with cardamom-scented Quorn™

This is a sure-fire success with vegetarians; do make sure the cauliflower is fresh with tightly closed florets. Quorn is available in most supermarkets and health-food stores. Vegans might prefer to use soya mince instead.

Great Indian Feasts

Serves 4

10 green cardamom pods, bruised
1 teaspoon salt
1 medium-sized cauliflower
4 tablespoons sunflower or olive oil
1 teaspoon cumin seeds
1 large red onion, finely chopped
2 teaspoons ginger purée
2 teaspoons garlic purée
450g/1lb minced Quorn
½ teaspoon ground turmeric
2 teaspoons ground coriander
½ teaspoon ground cumin
½–1 teaspoon chilli powder
200g/7oz chopped canned tomatoes with the juice
1 tablespoon tomato purée
1 tablespoon snipped chives
½ teaspoon black mustard seeds
½ teaspoon onion seeds
1 Thai red chilli, chopped (seeded, if liked)
sprigs of coriander, to garnish

Fill a medium-sized saucepan with hot water until two-thirds full and add 6 of the bruised cardamom pods and a pinch of the salt. Add the whole cauliflower, bring back to the boil and cook for 5–6 minutes. Drain and plunge in iced water to prevent further cooking.

Meanwhile, heat 3 tablespoons of the oil over a low heat and add the remaining cardamom pods and the cumin. Let them sizzle for 15–20 seconds and add the chopped onion. Raise the heat to medium and fry the onion until soft, but not brown.

Add the ginger and garlic and cook for 2–3 minutes, then add the minced Quorn. Stir-fry the Quorn until it begins to brown then reduce the heat to low. Add the turmeric, coriander, cumin and chilli powder. Stir-fry for about a minute and add the tomatoes, tomato purée and remaining salt. Raise the heat slightly and stir-fry for 2–3 minutes, the reduce the heat to low, cover the pan and cook for 5–6 minutes. Remove from the heat, stir in the chives and allow the Quorn to cool slightly.

Drain the cauliflower well and place it on a board, stem side up. Fill all the cavity between the stems with cooked Quorn; this should be as tightly packed as possible. Next, turn the cauliflower over and gently pull the florets apart (you need to be extra careful not to break the florets) and fill with as much Quorn as possible. Reserve the remaining Quorn.

Heat the remaining oil (a wok is best for this stage of cooking) over a medium heat and add the mustard seeds; when they start popping add the onion seeds and the chilli.

Place the cauliflower on the seasoned oil, the right way up, and let it cook, uncovered, for 2–3 minutes. Carefully turn it over and cook for a further 2–3 minutes.

Turn the cauliflower again and spread the reserved Quorn round it. Cover the pan, reduce the heat to very low and cook for 10–15 minutes or until the cauliflower is tender but still firm. Transfer it to a serving dish and spread some of the Quorn on it and arrange the remaininder around it. Garnish with the sprigs of coriander, cut into quarters and serve.

Stuffed breasts of chicken in almond sauce

A luscious almond sauce, perfumed with golden saffron combined with the bouquet of rose water and spiced with ginger and nutmeg, characterises this supreme korma which comes from the courtly cuisine of India. The list of ingredients may seem long, but it is really quite simple to prepare.

Serves 4

large pinch of saffron
   threads, pounded
2 tablespoons hot milk
4 chicken breast fillets,
   skinned
50g/2oz whole milk yogurt
2.5cm/1in piece root ginger,
   finely grated
4 large garlic cloves, crushed
   to a pulp
½ teaspoon salt
½ teaspoon chilli powder

FOR THE STUFFING
25g/1oz mild Cheddar
   cheese, grated
6 dried, ready-to-eat
   apricots, finely chopped
15g/1/2oz raw cashew nuts,
   chopped
½ teaspoon freshly grated
   nutmeg
2 green chillies, finely
   chopped

FOR THE SAUCE
50g/2oz blanched almonds
   soaked for 15 minutes in
   150ml/5fl oz boiling water
50g/2oz unsalted butter
1 tablespoon sunflower oil

Soak the saffron in the hot milk for 5–7 minutes. Wrap each chicken breast loosely in clingfilm and flatten with a meat mallet or a rolling pin.

Whisk the yogurt until smooth and add the saffron milk followed by the ginger, garlic, salt and chilli powder. Pour this marinade over the chicken and rub in gently. Cover and refrigerate for at least 2 hours.

Mix all the ingredients for the stuffing. Lay the pieces of marinated chicken on a flat surface and place some stuffing on one side of each breast, dividing them equally among the four. Roll up the meat and tie it with a piece of string in a criss-cross fashion.

In a heavy-based pan, melt 15g/½oz of the butter over a medium heat and place the stuffed chicken breasts side by side in a single layer. Cook until the underside is opaque (about 2 minutes); turn them over carefully and let the other side go opaque. Then, turn the heat right down, pour in any leftover marinade, cover and cook gently for 25 minutes, turning the breasts around the pan occasionally.

Place half the remaining butter and the oil over a medium heat and sauté the onion, ginger and garlic for 3–4 minutes. Remove from the heat and cool slightly then purée them along with the almonds and the water in which they were soaked.

1 small onion, finely chopped
2.5cm/1in piece root ginger,
    roughly chopped
4 large garlic cloves, roughly
chopped
½ teaspoon garam masala
¼ teaspoon freshly grated
    nutmeg
small pinch of saffron
    threads, pounded and
    soaked in 1 tablespoon
    hot milk
½ teaspoon salt
150ml/5fl oz single cream
1 tablespoon rose water
toasted flaked almonds,
    to garnish
Cardamom-scented Basmati
Rice, to serve (page 133)

Next, melt the last quantity of butter over a low heat and add the garam masala and nutmeg. Let them sizzle gently for 15–20 seconds and add the puréed ingredients and saffron milk. Add the salt and cream, then the chicken, along with all the cooking juices. Cover and simmer gently for 10–12 minutes, stirring once or twice.

Remove from the heat and stir in the rose water. Serve garnished with the toasted almonds and accompanied by Cardamom–scented Basmati Rice.

Mridula Baljekar

Fisherman's pie with coconut and coriander sauce

This recipe is inspired by a dish called Fisherman's Platter which we serve in my restaurant. The combination of fish and prawns, together with the carefully chosen combination of spices, produce a sensational dish which is also nourishing and extremely satisfying. You can make it in one large, deep ovenproof dish or in individual dishes.

Serves 6

FOR THE TOPPING
750g/1lb potatoes
6 garlic cloves, chopped
½ teaspoon salt
50g/2oz butter
4 tablespoons single cream
½ teaspoon black pepper
¼ teaspoon grated nutmeg
1 tablespoon snipped chives
1 fresh red chilli, chopped
125g/4oz soft white
   breadcrumbs

FOR THE FILLING
4 tablespoons light olive oil
1 large onion, finely chopped
2.5cm/1in piece root ginger,
   finely grated
2 green chillies, chopped
1 tablespoon garlic purée
2 teaspoons ground coriander
½ teaspoon ground fennel
   seeds
½ teaspoon chilli powder
400ml/14fl oz coconut milk
175g/6oz cod fillet, cut into
   1cm/½ in cubes
175g/6oz salmon fillet, cut into
   1cm/½ in cubes
450g/1lb cooked, peeled prawns
2 tablespoons chopped fresh
   coriander leaves

Peel and quarter or halve the potatoes according to their size. Put into a saucepan with the garlic and salt and add enough water to cover them. Bring to the boil, reduce the heat slightly and cook until the potatoes are tender. Reserve 200ml/7fl oz of the cooking liquid and drain the potatoes well, then mash them with 25g/1oz of the butter and the remaining ingredients for the topping, except the breadcrumbs. Using a fork, blend in the reserved cooking liquid and set the potato mixture aside.

Preheat the oven to 230°C/450°F/Gas Mark 8.

To prepare the filling, heat the oil over a medium heat and fry the onion, ginger, chilli and garlic until the onion is soft (about 5 minutes).

Add the coriander, fennel and chilli powder, cook for about a minute and purée them in a blender with the coconut milk. Return the mixture to the pan and add the fish, prawns and coriander leaves. Mix thoroughly then divide the mixture into 6 individual baking dishes (approximately 15 x 10 x 5cm/6 x 4 x 2in) or one large ovenproof dish (approximately 30 x 23 x 7.5cm/12 x 9 x 3in).

Pipe or spread the potato mixture over the filling. Melt the remaining butter and mix with the breadcrumbs. Spread it over the potato and bake in the centre of the oven for 30–35 minutes or until the top is brown. Serve accompanied by Spiced Savoy Cabbage with Chestnuts (page 170).

Nine-jewelled korma

The confetti of colours, the contrast of flavours and textures and the subtle richness will make this dish the central attraction at any dinner party. Nine types of fruits and vegetables are used in one dish which was created as a tribute to the nine courtiers of the Mogul Emperor Akbar.

Serves 4–5

1 large onion, roughly chopped
90g/3oz raw cashew nut pieces
90g/3oz natural yogurt
3 tablespoons light olive oil or sunflower oil
1 green chilli, finely chopped (seeded, if wished)
50g/2oz each of red, green and yellow peppers, seeded and diced
50g/2oz frozen garden peas
50g/2oz frozen sweetcorn kernels
125g/4oz carrots, diced and blanched
125g/4oz green beans, cut into 2.5cm/1in lengths and blanched
125g/4oz paneer, finely diced
¼ teaspoon ground turmeric
1 teaspoon salt
90ml/3fl oz canned coconut milk
90g/3oz canned fruit cocktail, drained (use fruits such as pineapple, grapes, peaches and cherries)
2 tablespoons single cream
Pilau Rice with Toasted Pine Nuts (page 174) or plain naan, to serve

Put the onion into a saucepan and add 125ml/4fl oz water. Bring it to the boil, reduce the heat slightly and cook until the onion is soft. Allow to cool.

Meanwhile, soak the cashews in 150ml/¼ pint boiling water for 20 minutes then purée them along with the water in which they were soaked.

Next, purée the onion, add the yogurt and blend together then mix thoroughly with the puréed cashews. Set aside.

In a heavy-based saucepan, heat the oil over a medium heat and sauté the chilli for 35–40 seconds.

Add the peppers, peas, sweetcorn, carrots and green beans and continue to sauté for a further 2–3 minutes.

Add the paneer and turmeric and sauté for a further 1–2 minutes then add the puréed ingredients. Stir in the salt, cover and reduce the heat to very low. Simmer for 8–9 minutes until the vegetables are tender but still firm.

Add the coconut milk and simmer for 1–2 minutes.

Transfer the korma to a serving dish and add the fruit cocktail, then lightly fork through the vegetables. Swirl the cream on top and serve accompanied by Pilau Rice with Toasted Pine Nuts or plain naan.

Mridula Baljekar

Roast turkey marinated in spice-laced yogurt

A complete break from the traditional way of preparing and roasting, this Christmas turkey with subtle spicing is sure to be a hit with all Indian food lovers. Try and choose a small bird because smaller ones will absorb the flavours right down to the bones. If necessary, cooking two small birds will produce better results than one large. Unlike the traditional method, you need to remove the skin from the turkey before marinating it. It is much quicker and easier to use a cloth (to prevent slipping) to pull back the skin.

Serves 6

1 small turkey (3.5kg/8lb),
  skin removed
juice of 1 lemon
1½ teaspoons salt
90g/3oz whole milk natural
  yogurt
1½ tablespoons garlic purée
1½ teaspoons ginger purée
2 teaspoons garam masala
1 teaspoon ground turmeric
1 teaspoon chilli powder or
  to taste
50ml/2fl oz sunflower oil
125ml/5fl oz dry white wine
50g/2oz butter, melted

FOR THE STUFFING
450g/1lb minced chicken
1 teaspoon salt
1 teaspoon garlic paste
1 teaspoon ginger paste
1 teaspoon garam masala
½ teaspoon freshly milled
  black pepper
2 tablespoons chopped fresh
  coriander leaves

Lay the turkey on its back. Make 3 deep incisions right across each breast, the outer and inner legs and thighs and the wings.

Rub the lemon juice and salt all over the turkey and set aside for 30 minutes.

Mix all the ingredients together for the marinade, except the wine and butter, and pour over the bird. Rub it well into the slits, turn it over and rub the marinade on the back. Transfer the bird to a large dish, cover with foil or clingfilm and refrigerate for 36–48 hours. Leave at room temperature overnight on Christmas Eve.

Just before you put the bird in the oven, mix all the ingredients for the stuffing together and fill the stomach cavity with the stuffing. Tie up the bird securely with string and place it on a deep roasting tin, breast side down. Pour 200ml/7fl oz hot water into the tin (but not over the bird) and cover with foil, making sure that the foil does not touch the bird. Make sure it is completely sealed by folding the foil well over the edges of the roasting tin. Cook the bird just below the centre of a preheated oven (200°C/400°F/Gas Mark 6) for 45 minutes. Reduce the temperature to 180°C/350°F/Gas Mark 4 and cook for a further 45 minutes.

1 tablespoon chopped fresh
  mint leaves or 1 teaspoon
  dried mint

FOR THE GRAVY
1 tablespoon chick pea flour
  (besan)
50ml/2fl oz dry white wine
1 tablespoon snipped chives
salt and pepper to taste

Spiced Savoy Cabbage
  with Chestnuts, to serve
  (page 170)

Remove the foil and carefully turn the bird over on its back. Pour the wine evenly all over, taking particular care to moisten the breast meat and legs. Cook for 10 minutes, then baste generously with the melted butter. Cook for a further 30 minutes basting every 10 minutes with the pan juices. Remove from the heat and allow to rest for 10–15 minutes.

Transfer the turkey to a serving plate and strain off all the cooking juices from the tin into a measuring jug. You should have approx 425ml/15fl oz of juices, but, if not, make it up to this amount by adding cold water.

Make a paste with the chick pea flour and a little water and blend it into the turkey stock. Cook over a medium heat, beating it with a wire whisk to prevent lumps forming. Add the wine and chives, cook for a further minute or so. Season to taste and remove from the heat. Serve with Spiced Savoy Cabbage with Chestnuts.

Mridula Baljekar

Baked minced Quorn™ with fried onion purée

This is an adaptation from one of the original recipes in my *Complete Indian Cookbook* where I used minced lamb. This vegetarian version using Quorn is delicious as well as nutritious. Quorn is a vegetable protein which is high in dietary fibre and free from cholesterol. Firm or extra-firm tofu makes a good alternative to Quorn.

Great Indian Feasts

Serves 4

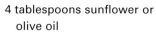

4 tablespoons sunflower or
  olive oil
1 large onion, roughly
  chopped
2.5cm/1in piece root ginger,
  peeled and roughly
  chopped
1 dried red chilli, broken up
125g/4oz whole milk plain
  yogurt
½ teaspoon cumin seeds
½ teaspoon onion seeds
2 teaspoons garlic purée
½ teaspoon ground turmeric
½ teaspoon chilli powder or
  to taste
1 teaspoon ground coriander
450g/1lb minced Quorn
300ml/½ pint warm water
1 teaspoon salt
1 tablespoon tomato purée
½ teaspoon garam masala
2 tablespoons coarsely
  chopped fresh coriander
  leaves
4 large eggs
parsley or coriander sprigs,
  to garnish
naan or garlic bread, to serve

Heat two tablespoons of the oil over a medium heat and sauté the onion, ginger and chilli for 4–5 minutes until lightly browned. Remove from the heat and purée them with the yogurt. Set aside.

Heat the remaining oil over a medium heat and add the cumin and onion seeds. Let them sizzle for 15–20 seconds, reduce the heat to low and add the garlic. Sauté until the garlic begins to brown and add the turmeric, chilli powder and coriander. Cook gently for 30–40 seconds and add the Quorn. Raise the heat to medium again and sauté the Quorn for 4–5 minutes, stirring frequently. Add the water and salt, stir and bring it to the boil. Cover the pan, reduce the heat to low and simmer for 15–20 minutes, stirring occasionally.

Add the blended ingredients, tomato purée, garam masala and coriander leaves. Stir thoroughly and simmer, uncovered, for 1–2 minutes.

Preheat the oven to 190°C/375°F/Gas Mark 5. Transfer the Quorn into a shallow ovenproof dish and make 4 hollows, about 2.5cm/1in apart. Break an egg into each hollow and bake in the centre of the oven for 25–30 minutes or until the eggs are set.

Garnish with the parsley or coriander and serve with naan or garlic bread.

Fish in aromatic tomato sauce

This recipe is from my book *Secrets From An Indian Kitchen*. I have chosen it because this is the kind of fish curry we had at home during special occasions and weddings. In the north-eastern part of the country, where I grew up, fish is a standard item on the menu. The fish found in Indian water is firm, dense and delicious. My choice here is tuna steak, but you could use any firm fish.

Serves 4

4 tuna steaks (700 g/1½ lb)
1 teaspoon salt or to taste
2.5 cm/1 in cube of root ginger, roughly chopped
4 large garlic cloves, roughly chopped
2–4 green chillies, seeded and roughly chopped
4 tablespoons sunflower oil
1 large onion, finely chopped
1 teaspoon ground aniseed
1 teaspoon ground turmeric
200 ml/7 fl oz chopped canned tomatoes, sieved
½ teaspoon black mustard seeds
½ teaspoon onion seeds
8-10 fenugreek seeds
2 tablespoons chopped coriander leaves
boiled basmati rice, to serve

Cut each steak into 3-4 thick slices and sprinkle half teaspoon of the salt. Set aside. If you are using frozen fish, thaw completely and pat dry with absorbent paper first.

Purée the ginger, garlic and chillies in a blender, adding a little water if necessary.

In a sauté or other suitable pan, heat 3 tablespoons of the oil over a medium heat. Add the onion and fry, stirring regularly, until it is soft and has a tinge of brown, then add the puréed ingredients. Continue to cook for 30–40 seconds, then add the ground aniseed and turmeric. Stir-fry for 1 minute and add the sieved tomatoes and the remaining salt. Cook for 2-3 minutes and add 150 ml/5 fl oz lukewarm water. Stir and let the sauce bubble gently for a minute or so, then add the fish. Cover the pan, reduce the heat to low and cook for 10–12 minutes.

In a wok, small saucepan or a steel ladle, heat the remaining oil over a medium heat. When hot, add the mustard seeds, followed by the onion seeds and then switch off the heat source. Next, add the fenugreek seeds and let them sizzle for 15–20 seconds. Fold in the spice mixture along with the flavoured oil into the tomato sauce. Keep the pan covered until you are ready to serve. Serve with boiled basmati rice garnished with the coriander leaves.

Mridula Baljekar

Secrets from an Indian Kitchen by Mridula Beljekar, Pavilion Books (2003)

Spiced savoy cabbage with chestnuts

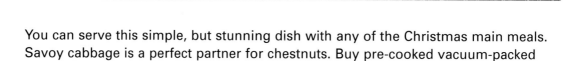

You can serve this simple, but stunning dish with any of the Christmas main meals. Savoy cabbage is a perfect partner for chestnuts. Buy pre-cooked vacuum-packed chestnuts for best results. At Christmas, in my restaurant, we serve this with Slow–cooked Lamb Shanks.

Serves 6

25g/1oz unsalted butter
½ teaspoon cumin seeds
½ teaspoon fennel seeds
2–3 large garlic cloves, finely
  chopped
1 large Savoy cabbage, finely
  shredded
150g/5oz cooked chestnuts,
  sliced
salt, to taste
2 tablespoons white wine
  vinegar
4 tablespoons double cream
freshly milled black pepper

Melt the butter gently in a heavy-based pan and add the cumin, fennel and garlic. Cook gently until the garlic begins to brown.

Add the cabbage, chestnuts and salt. Stir them around to mix thoroughly then add the vinegar. Stir over a medium-high heat, then reduce the heat and cook for 4–5 minutes until the cabbage is tender but firm.

Add the double cream and plenty of freshly milled black pepper. Stir well and remove from the heat.

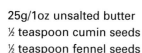

Oven-roasted potatoes with mixed peppers

In Indian cooking, even the humble potato can offer you a bouquet of flavours. These are highlighted in different degrees according to the combination of spices and method of cooking. In this simple recipe, roasted poppy and sesame seeds provide a delicious nuttiness. Chargrilled peppers accentuate both its depth of flavour and visual appeal.

Serves 4

750g/1lb potatoes
1 small red pepper
1 small green pepper
4 tablespoons sunflower oil
½ teaspoon black mustard
  seeds
½ teaspoon cumin seeds
1 teaspoon salt
1½ tablespoons white poppy
  seeds
1 tablespoon sesame seeds
3–4 dried red chillies, roughly
  chopped
rice, bread or a main dish
  to serve

Preheat the oven to 230°C/450°F/Gas Mark 8. Peel and cut the potatoes into 2.5cm/1in cubes. Leave to soak for 10 minutes, then drain and dry with a clean tea towel.

Meanwhile, grill the peppers until the skin is charred. You can do this either under a hot grill or on the hob, using a wire rack directly on the gas burner. Turn the peppers regularly in either case. It will take 5–6 minutes for them to char. Place them in a plastic bag for 15–20 minutes.

In a roasting tin, heat the oil over a medium heat and add the mustard seeds. As soon as they start crackling, add the cumin seeds, then the potatoes and salt. Increase the heat to medium and fry the potatoes for 3–4 minutes until browned, then place the tin in the centre of the oven. Cook for 12–15 minutes.

Remove the peppers from the bag and peel away the skin. Remove the pith and the seeds and cut the peppers into 2.5cm/1in cubes.

Preheat a small pan over medium heat. When hot, reduce the heat to low and dry roast the poppy and sesame seeds for 45–50 seconds until they begin to release the roasted aroma. Do not allow them to brown. Once cool, grind them in a coffee or spice mill or pestle and mortar.

When the potatoes are ready, add the peppers and the ground ingredients. Mix thoroughly and return to the oven for 3–4 minutes. Remove and serve immediately.

Mridula Baljekar

Garlic and rosemary naan with truffle oil

This is a really simplified version of making naan at home. You can use the dough to make plain naan or use all kinds of topping before baking. Garlic and rosemary with truffle oil is a very special topping and one that is ideal for the festive season or any other special occasion. Instead of ghee (clarified butter) or butter, I have used milk to make the dough which makes the naans soft and moist.

Makes 8

450g/1lb self-raising flour
2 teaspoons sugar
1 teaspoon salt
1 teaspoon baking powder
4 tablespoons truffle oil plus
　a little extra for brushing
250ml/9fl oz whole milk,
　warmed
vegetable oil, for brushing
4–6 garlic cloves, finely
　chopped or minced
few sprigs of rosemary,
　stripped off the stems

In a large mixing bowl sift the flour, sugar, salt and baking powder together. Add the oil and rub in well with your fingertips. Gradually add the warmed milk and mix until a soft dough is formed. Transfer it to a pastry board and knead for 5–6 minutes until smooth, soft and pliable. Cover the bowl with clingfilm or a damp cloth and set aside for 20–25 minutes.

Divide the dough into 8 equal-sized portions and flatten them into thick cakes by rotating them between your palms. Cover them again and set aside for 10–15 minutes. Preheat the grill to high for 8–10 minutes and line a grill pan with a piece of foil and brush well with some oil.

Roll each flattened cake into a 13cm/5in-diameter disc and pull the lower end gently to form a teardrop shape if you wish to make the traditional shape. Roll them carefully again, maintaining the teardrop shape, to about 23cm/9in. Alternatively, roll them out to 23cm/9in circles. Sprinkle a little chopped garlic and a few rosemary leaves over each naan and gently press them down with your fingers.

Place the prepared naan on the lined grill pan and grill 13cm/5in below the heat source for about 1½ minutes until puffed. Watch carefully and, as soon as brown spots appear on the surface, turn it over and grill the other side until browned lightly. Place the cooked naan on a clean tea towel and brush lightly with truffle oil then wrap it up while you finish cooking the rest.

Shiitake mushrooms in savoury onion sauce

Slices of shiitake mushrooms wrapped in a delicately spiced onion sauce are a pure delight! Cultivated button mushrooms can be used instead, but I find it hard to resist the magical aura of shiitake!

Serves 4

350g/12oz shiitake
  mushrooms
3–4 tablespoons sunflower
  or olive oil
1 large red onion, finely
  chopped
2 teaspoons garlic purée or
  4–5 large garlic cloves,
  crushed to a pulp
1 teaspoon ginger purée or
  1cm/½in piece root ginger,
  finely grated
½ teaspoon ground turmeric
½ teaspoon chilli powder
1 teaspoon ground coriander
½ teaspoon ground cumin
salt to taste
1 tablespoon tomato purée
1–2 tablespoons chopped
  fresh coriander leaves

Wipe the mushrooms with a damp kitchen towel and slice them thickly.

Heat the oil over a medium heat and fry the onion until soft. Add the garlic and fry for about a minute. Next, add the turmeric, chilli powder, coriander and cumin. Cook gently for 30–40 seconds and add the mushrooms, salt and tomato purée. Pour in 600ml/1 pint warm water and stir to mix everything thoroughly. Bring it to the boil, reduce the heat to low and cover the pan. Cook for 15–20 minutes, stirring occasionally.

Stir in the coriander leaves and remove from the heat.

Mridula Baljekar

Pilau rice with toasted pine nuts

Nuts are often used to garnish pilaus and biryanis and I think pine nuts exude a sense of the exotic.

Serves 4

225g/8oz basmati rice
40g/1½oz ghee or unsalted
   butter
5cm/2in piece of cinnamon
   stick
4 green cardamom pods,
   bruised
4 cloves
½ teaspoon black
   peppercorns
2 bay leaves, crumpled
25g/1oz raw cashews
   (optional)
¼ teaspoon ground turmeric
½ teaspoon salt
1 tablespoon pine nuts

Wash the rice in several changes of cold water then soak it in cold water for 15–20 minutes. Drain thoroughly.

In a heavy non-stick saucepan, heat the ghee or butter over a low heat and add the cinnamon, cardamom, cloves, peppercorns, bay leaves and cashews (if using). Stir-fry the ingredients gently for 25–30 seconds and add the rice, turmeric and salt. Stir-fry for 2–3 minutes and pour in 500ml/18fl oz hot water. Bring it to the boil and let it cook, uncovered, for 2–3 minutes. Reduce the heat to low, cover the pan tightly and cook for 7–8 minutes. Remove from the heat and let it stand for 5–6 minutes.

Meanwhile, preheat the grill to high and grill the pine nuts until they brown lightly. Fluff up the rice with a fork and transfer it to a serving dish. Scatter the toasted nuts on top and serve.

Great Indian Feasts

Christmas chutneys

An Indian meal is incomplete without those inviting, taste-bud-reviving little relishes, but there is much more to these tempting treats than the usually popular mango chutney and lime pickle.

In this section you will find chutneys which perhaps you may not have come across before because they come straight from my own family kitchen. The only exceptions are the Cranberry Chutney and the Rhubarb and Raisin Chutney. Having lived in England for more than half of my life, I have learned to adapt the recipes to include typical British produce. I fondly remember my mother carefully picking fresh fruits such as apricots and pineapples, plus herbs like mint and coriander, indigenous to the north–eastern region of India, from the garden and making mouthwatering relishes. These were sometimes sweetened with jaggery (unrefined palm sugar), salted with rock salt and soured with tamarind picked from the huge tamarind tree in our back garden. The relishes had the additional advantage of our homegrown garlic bulbs ... and fiery red and green chillies! When these were ground on the traditional grinding stone, the air filled with a magical aroma. Somehow, today's modern gadgets don't appear to have quite the same effect!

How to sterilise jars

Wash the jars in hot soapy water and dry with a clean cloth. Put them in the centre of a moderately hot (180°C/350°F/Gas Mark 4) oven for 8–10 minutes. It is best to fill the jars while they are still warm.

Spiced cranberry chutney

A fabulous do-ahead chutney which is absolutely yummy. Besides serving it with Turkey and Guinea Fowl Kebabs (page 146), try it with venison and pork sausages and, indeed, with traditional roast turkey or my Roast Turkey Marinated in Spice-laced Yogurt (page 166).

Makes about 450g/1lb

450g/1lb fresh cranberries
2 tablespoons olive oil
½ teaspoon black mustard seeds
½ teaspoon cumin seeds
2–3 star anise
1–2 fresh red chillies, chopped
½ teaspoon hot chilli powder
½ teaspoon ground cumin
50g/2oz seedless raisins
90g/3oz light brown sugar
½ teaspoon salt

Using the pulse action in your food processor, chop the cranberries.

In a heavy saucepan, heat the oil over a medium heat. When hot, but not smoking, add the mustard seeds, followed by the cumin and star anise. Let them sizzle for 15–20 seconds.

Add the fresh chillies and cook for 30 seconds, then stir in the chilli powder and ground cumin.

Add the raisins, cranberries, sugar and salt. Mix everything together and cover the pan with a lid. Reduce the heat slightly and cook for 6–8 minutes. Remove from the heat and allow to cool. Store in sterilised jars for 6–8 weeks.

Mridula Baljekar

Apricot chutney

You can make this glorious chutney a month before Christmas. It is good with all kinds of Christmas food such as roast turkey or pork, cold turkey sandwiches and all kinds of game birds.

Makes about 450g/1lb

450g/1lb dried ready-to-eat apricots
275g/10oz soft light brown sugar
425ml/15fl oz white wine vinegar
2.5cm/1in piece root ginger, finely grated
1 teaspoon chilli powder
1 teaspoon salt
450ml/16fl oz water
2.5cm/1in piece of cinnamon stick
½ teaspoon coriander seeds
½ teaspoon fennel seeds
1 teaspoon cumin seeds

Chop the apricots finely and put into a saucepan with the rest of the ingredients, except the coriander, fennel and cumin seeds. Place over a high heat and bring to the boil. Reduce the heat to low and simmer, uncovered, until the chutney has thickened to a stiff consistency (about 30–35 minutes).

Meanwhile, preheat a small heavy pan over a medium heat. Reduce the heat to low and add the whole spices. Stir them around for about a minute until they release their aroma. Remove and let cool, then crush them finely in a mortar and pestle or a coffee mill. When the chutney is ready, stir in the spice mixture, cool and transfer to a sterilised jar. Store in the fridge.

Great Indian Feasts

Rhubarb and raisin chutney

Rhubarb chutney is a real taste-bud reviver with its amalgamation of exciting flavours. It is excellent with all kinds of fried and grilled snacks.

Serves 4–6

1kg/2lb rhubarb
4 tablespoons sunflower oil
¼ teaspoon mustard seeds
¼ teaspoon cumin seeds
¼ teaspoon fennel seeds
¼ teaspoon onion seeds
5–6 fenugreek seeds
2.5cm/1in piece root ginger, grated or 2 teaspoons ginger purée
1–3 teaspoons chilli powder
2 teaspoons ground cumin
1 teaspoon salt
125–150g/4–5oz soft brown sugar
50g/2oz seedless raisins

Wash and skin the rhubarb, if necessary (if the skin is coarse). Cut into 1cm/½in pieces.

Heat the oil over a low heat. When hot, add the mustards seeds; as soon as they start popping, add the cumin, fennel, onion and fenugreek seeds. Let them crackle for 15–20 seconds and add the ginger. Fry gently for 1 minute, then add the chilli powder and cumin.

Immediately follow with the rhubarb, salt and sugar. Stir over a medium heat for 2–3 minutes, then reduce the heat to low, cover the pan with a piece of moist greaseproof paper, then with a lid. Cook for 8–10 minutes.

Remove and discard the greaseproof paper and add the raisins. Cook over a low heat, uncovered, for 12–15 minutes until thickened. Stir occasionally. Remove and let it cool completely, then store in a dry screwtop jar. It will keep well in the fridge up to two weeks.

Mridula Baljekar

Pineapple chutney

Succulent golden pineapple, rich and creamy cashew nuts and plump raisins are flavoured with a classic mix of east Indian spices. You can vary the combination by using dried dates instead of raisins and use dried apricots or peaches instead of the cashews.

Makes 350g/12oz

1 small ripe, firm pineapple
4 tablespoons sunflower
  or vegetable oil
¼ teaspoon black mustard
  seeds
¼ teaspoon cumin seeds
¼ teaspoon fennel seeds
¼ teaspoon onion seeds
5–6 fenugreek seeds
1½ teaspoons ground cumin
1 teaspoon ground coriander
1–3 teaspoons chilli powder
25g/1oz seedless raisins
25g/1oz unsalted natural
  cashews
1 tablespoon finely chopped
  crystallised ginger
1½ teaspoons salt
125g/4oz soft brown sugar
1 tablespoon white wine
  or cider vinegar

Quarter the pineapple, peel, then remove the eyes with a small sharp knife. Remove the central core and cut the quarters into smallish chunks.

Heat the oil over a medium heat and add the mustard seeds. As soon as they start crackling, add the cumin, fennel, onion and fenugreek seeds. Let them all sizzle for 5–10 seconds.

Add the pineapple and the remaining ingredients, except the vinegar, stir and reduce the heat to low. Cover the pan and cook gently for 45–50 minutes, stirring occasionally.

Add the vinegar, stir and remove from the heat. The pineapple should remain in small soft chunks. When the chutney has cooled, transfer to a sterilised jar. It will keep well without refrigeration for 4–5 weeks.

Great Indian Feasts

Apple and mint chutney

The soft green appearance of this chutney matches the delicate taste and flavour amazingly well. Eat with a plain piece of toast or a savoury biscuit or with any kind of spicy snack.

Serves 4–5

90g/3oz desiccated coconut
1 eating apple, such as a
  Granny Smith
3 tablespoons chopped fresh
  mint leaves
3–4 tablespoons roughly
  chopped fresh coriander
  leaves and stalks
5mm/¼in piece root ginger,
  chopped
1 garlic clove, chopped
¾ teaspoon salt
½ teaspoon sugar
1 tablespoon lemon juice

Soak the coconut in 175ml/6fl oz boiling water for 10–15 minutes.

Core, but do not peel the apple. Chop it roughly.

Place the coconut, along with the water in which it was soaked, in a blender. Add all the remaining ingredients and blend until smooth; transfer to a serving dish. Serve at room temperature. This chutney is best eaten fresh.

Mridula Baljekar

desserts and sweetmeats

Choosing the dessert is a skilful task with any cuisine. Once the starter and the main course have been selected, the dessert has to complement them. Choosing the wrong dessert is likely to upset the entire balance of the meal.

It is difficult to resist the temptation of a good dessert –in fact, it is easy to succumb to unashamed gluttony! It is, however, important to think of the other courses on the menu when you select the dessert so that you can make the right choice in terms of taste, flavour, texture and, to a certain extent, the colour. Rich main courses should be followed by a light and refreshing dessert and, if the main course is reasonably free of rich ingredients, then an indulgent dessert is appropriate and enjoyable.

Most Indian desserts are dairy based and they tend to be quite heavy. After a traditional Indian meal, light, fruit-based desserts, in my experience, have proved to be more popular. The lightness and tanginess of these dishes offset nicely the powerful aftertaste of spiced food. Desserts have never been important to an Indian meal, but on a special occasion, it would seem incomplete without one.

In India, we opt for fresh fruits rather than a heavy dessert. Although we have a fine range of sweets, these are more frequently eaten with tea and coffee, just like biscuits and cream cakes in the West. Sweets are also associated with festivals because they are considered to be 'foods of the Gods' – they are made and offered to god first, then exchanged between friends and relations.

In this section, you will find a small selection of desserts to complement your Christmas meal. The light and tangy Pomegranate Sorbet and Brandy and Port Jelly with Exotic Fruits will nicely offset the powerful after-taste of spiced food. In India, sweets are also associated with festivals because they are considered to be 'the food of the gods'. Festivals are times for sharing a common tie of religious and social beliefs. Sweets are made and offered to the gods first, then exchanged between friends and relations. The Goan Christmas Cake and the Small Coconut Cakes are ideal for this purpose.

Brandy and port jelly with exotic fruits

This deliciously intoxicating dessert comes from Imperial India. Teamed with fresh exotic fruits, this will make a fantastic end to your spicy Christmas lunch.

Serves 6

125ml/4fl oz brandy
125ml/4fl oz water
50ml/2fl oz port
125ml/4fl oz water
5cm/2in piece of cinnamon
   stick, broken up
6 cloves
1 teaspoon whole allspice
   berries
50g/2oz caster sugar
1 packet orange-flavoured
   jelly
150ml/5fl oz fresh whole milk
150ml/5fl oz double cream
450g/1lb diced mixed fruits
   such as mango, papaya
   and kiwi and the seeds of
   half a pomegranate,
   to serve

Put all the ingredients, except the jelly, milk and cream, in a saucepan and bring to the boil. Cover and simmer for 10 minutes and remove from the heat.

Cut the jelly into cubes and add to the spiced liquid. Stir until dissolved. Cover and set aside for 10–15 minutes.

Strain the mixture into a bowl and stand the bowl in iced water. When the mixture is lukewarm, stir in the milk.

Whisk the cream until it is thick, but not stiff. Gradually add the jelly while still whisking.

Rinse out a 600ml/1 pint ring mould with cold water. If you do not have a ring mould use a pudding basin. Pour in the punch and refrigerate for 6–7 hours or until set. Turn out on to a serving plate and fill the centre of the ring mould with the fruits. Scatter the pomegranate seeds on top.

Mridula Baljekar

Goan Christmas cake

A classic example of the intermingling of cultures, this cake is Portuguese in origin and was introduced to Goa during the period of colonisation. Known as Bibinca, you may think this is a sinful treat! But, at Christmas time I think we can ignore the calories and enjoy the delicious goodies that go into making this cake. You can make this a week in advance and store in the fridge or, if you have time, even on Christmas Eve! Serve at room temperature.

Serves 8

450g/1lb caster sugar
250ml/9fl oz water
250g/9oz plain flour
1 whole nutmeg, grated
1 teaspoon ground cinnamon
12 medium egg yolks
2.5 litres/4 pints coconut milk
200g/7oz ghee or unsalted
   butter, melted

TO DECORATE
2 tablespoons apricot jam
3 tablespoons dark rum
10–12 walnut halves
10–12 whole blanched
   almonds
6 dried ready-to-eat apricots
6 glacé cherries, halved
1 tablespoon dried coconut
   flakes

Put the sugar and the water into a pan and heat gently until the sugar has dissolved. Remove from the heat and set aside to cool.

Mix the flour, nutmeg and cinnamon together.

Beat the egg yolks until light and creamy. Stir in the flour and spice mixture then beat in the cold sugar syrup.

Gradually add the coconut milk and beat until you have a smooth batter. Cover and set aside for 1 hour.

Preheat the grill to medium and the oven to 200°C/400°/ Gas Mark 6.

Heat 2 tablespoons melted ghee in a 20cm/8in frying pan and spread 150ml/5fl oz of the batter over the base of the pan. Allow to set, then turn off the heat. Place the pancake under the grill and let it brown. Remove and spread 2 tablespoons melted ghee on the browned side.

Spread 150ml/5fl oz batter over the cooked pancake and brown under the grill as before. Continue making and stacking the pancakes and browning them under the grill until the batter is used up.

When the pancakes are ready, remove the entire cake and place in a 20cm/8in cake tin. If you use a frying pan with ovenproof handles, then there is no need to transfer the stacked pancakes to a cake tin. As soon as the last pancake is ready, place the tin or frying pan straight into the oven. Bake in the centre of the oven for 15 minutes or until browned.

Heat the apricot jam and rum together and stir until the jam has melted. Brush the cake with a little of this mixture then stir in all the nuts and fruits except the coconut. You can decorate the top of the cake as you wish. Making a border with the walnut halves first and placing the flaked coconut in the middle of the cake will give you a good start.

This cake will keep well for 3–4 weeks. Store in the fridge, but serve at room temperature.

VARIATION
If you wish, you could use just shredded coconut to decorate the cake. Lightly brown the coconut under the grill, brush the centre of the cake with a little sieved apricot jam and place the coconut flakes on it. Dust the remaining area with icing sugar.

Small coconut cakes

These delicious little coconut cakes, known as Bolinho de Coco, come from Goa with a Portuguese influence. They are a perfect alternative to mince pies.

Makes 16

125g/4oz caster sugar
175ml/6fl oz water
6 cardamom pods, bruised
2.5cm/1in piece of cinnamon
    stick
175g/6oz desiccated coconut
1 tablespoon sesame seeds
50g/2oz raw cashews, lightly
    crushed with a rolling pin
1 tablespoon plain flour
2 medium eggs, beaten until
    light and fluffy
1 egg white, lightly beaten

Put the sugar, water, cardamom and cinnamon in a saucepan and bring to the boil. Reduce the heat to low and let it simmer for 6–7 minutes or until the syrup has thickened slightly.

Add the coconut and stir until the coconut has absorbed all the syrup. Remove from the heat, cool then remove the spices and stir in the sesame seeds, cashew nuts, flour and whole eggs.

Preheat the oven to 180°C/350°F/Gas Mark 4.

Divide the coconut mixture into 16 equal-sized portions and shape each into a smooth, flat, 1cm/½in-thick cake.

Line a baking sheet with greased greaseproof paper or non-stick baking parchment. Dip each cake in egg white and place on the baking sheet about 4cm/1½in apart. Bake in the centre of the oven for 25–30 minutes or until golden brown. Remove and cool on a wire rack. Store in an airtight container for up to two weeks.

Mridula Baljekar

Spiced-tea mousse with cardamom cream and lychees

Growing up in the north–eastern area of India where tea cultivation is one of the main industries, I have a weakness for a good cup of tea made with leaf tea. My mother always made us spiced tea in the winter and cold tea with scoops of ice cream in the summer. Based on my mother's spiced-tea recipe, I have developed THIS IDEA FOR A DESSERT WHICH I THINK IS DIVINE!

Serves 6

2 cinnamon sticks
6 cloves
4 black cardamom pods
4 teaspoons Assam leaf tea
50g/2oz granulated sugar
1½ leaves gelatine
1 egg
1 egg yolk
250ml/9fl oz double cream

FOR THE CARDAMOM CREAM
1 x 400g/14oz can lychees
8 cardamom pods
150ml/5fl oz double cream
2 tablespoons icing sugar, sieved
cocoa powder, to decorate

Boil 200ml/7fl oz water in a small pan, add the spices and simmer for 10 minutes. Add the tea and brew for 5 minutes, then strain. Mix in the sugar then leave to cool completely.

In a cup, sprinkle the gelatine with 2 tablespoons water and set aside until frothy. Place the cup over barely simmering water until the gelatine is clear.

Put the egg and egg yolk in a bowl and place over a pan of simmering water. Whisk until thick and creamy and the eggs hold a trail.

When the tea is cold, pour into the eggs and continue to whisk at the same time. Next whisk in the gelatine. Lightly whisk the cream and fold into the mixture. Pour into six moulds and set in the fridge.

To make the cardamom cream, drain the lychees and pour the syrup into a pan. Add the cardamom and boil until reduced to a third of its original volume. Remove and cool. Remove the cardamom pods.

Finely chop the lychees. Whip the cream until thick then add the icing sugar, lychees and reduced syrup.

Unmould the mousse on to a serving plate and place a generous topping of cardamom cream on top. Sprinkle the serving plate with sieved cocoa powder, if wished.

Cardamom-scented fresh pomegranate sorbet

Fresh Pomegranate Sorbet is easy to make and because of its light, clean and fresh taste, it is ideal as a palate reviver in between courses. You can buy pomegranate from supermarkets during season, which is Autumn through to late Spring. Choose them carefully and pick the ones which have a reddish tinge as they have those rich, ruby-coloured seeds which are extremely juicy and have a pleasant sweet, tart taste. I have used liquid glucose which prevents crystals forming. You can buy it from chemists.

Serves 4

8 large pomegranates
175g/6oz caster sugar
150ml/5fl oz cup water
2 star anise
4 green cardamom pods, bruised
3 teaspoons liquid glucose
Juice of one lemon
3 tablespoons grenadine
A few sprigs of fresh mint

Halve each pomegranate widthwise. Tap all around the skin with the handle of a large knife, holding the pomegranate half seed side down. This will loosen the seeds inside making it easier to remove the seeds. Next, peel off each pomegranate half like an orange and remove the seeds discarding the white pith next to the skin. Reserve a few seeds for decoration and purée the remainder in a blender. Put the puree in a sieve and place it over a large bowl, then push it through with a metal spoon to collect the juice. This should produce approximately 1.2 litre/2 pints/5 cups.

Put the sugar, water, star anise and cardamom pods into a saucepan and bring it to the boil, then simmer gently for 7–8 minutes. Remove from the heat, stir in the liquid glucose and allow to cool. Then remove the star anise and cardamom. Mix the cold syrup, lemon juice, grenadine and pomegranate juice together.

Pour the mixture into an ice cream box or other suitable container. Chill for approximately 4 hours. You could leave it overnight in the fridge then place the container in the coldest part of the freezer. Remove it from the freezer after 2 hours and whisk with an electric hand whisk or balloon whisk. Repeat this process twice more and place the container back in the freezer for 4–5 hours or overnight. Serve in stemmed glasses and decorate with the reserved seeds. Place a sprig of fresh mint in each glass.

An A–Z guide to Indian ingredients

ANISE (AJOWAN OR CARUM)

Anise, or aniseed, is native to India and looks rather like a celery seed. It is related to caraway and cumin, but the flavour is more akin to thyme. All Indian grocers stock anise and the seeds will keep for a number of years if stored in an airtight container. Only tiny amounts are used in pulses, fried snacks and fish dishes. Anise aids digestion and helps prevent flatulence.

ASAFOETIDA (HING)

Obtained from the resinous gum of a tropical plant, asafoetida can be bought from Indian stores in block or powder form. A block makes better sense as the flavour will keep well for several months. It should be used sparingly because of its strong flavour.

BAY LEAF (TEJ PATTA)

Bay leaves used in Indian cooking are obtained from the cassia tree. They are quite different from Western bay leaves, which come from the sweet bay laurel. Indian bay leaves are rarely available in the west and standard bay leaves have become a popular substitute.

BLACK PEPPERCORNS (KALI MIRCHI)

Fresh green berries are dried in the sun to obtain black pepper. Green berries come from the pepper vine native to monsoon forests of south-west India. Whole peppercorns will keep well in an airtight jar while ground black pepper loses the wonderful aromatic flavour very quickly. It is best to store whole pepper in a pepper mill and grind it only when required. Pepper is believed to be a good remedy for flatulence.

CARDAMOM (ELAICHI)

Cardamom has been used in Indian cooking since ancient times. Southern India produces an abundance of cardamom from where it found its way to Europe through the ancient spice route.

Whole cardamom pods are used to flavour rice and different types of sauces. Ground cardamom, used in many desserts and drinks, can be bought from most Asian stores. It is best to grind small quantities at home using a coffee mill. Prolonged storage dries out the essential natural oils which destroys the flavour. In India cardamom seeds are chewed after a meal as a mouth freshener. They are often coated in edible silver.

CHAPATTI FLOUR (ATTA)

This is a very fine wholewheat flour used to make all Indian unleavened bread. It is rich in dietary fibre because, unlike wholemeal flour, atta is produced by grinding the whole wheat kernel to a very fine powder.

CHICK PEA FLOUR (BESAN)

Made from skinned and ground chick peas, this is available from Indian stores. It has a nutty taste and cannot be substituted. It is also known as gram flour.

CHILLIES (MIRCHI)

It is difficult to judge the strength of chillies. Generally, the small thin ones are hot and the large fleshy ones tend to be milder. Most of the heat comes from the seeds, so it is best to remove them if you do not enjoy hot food. One way to do this is to slit the chilli lengthwise into half and scrape the seeds away under running water. Use a small knife for this. Another way is to hold the chilli between your palms and roll it for a few seconds. This will loosen the seeds. You can then slit the chilli without cutting it through completely and, holding the stem, simply shake out the seeds.

Always wash your hands thoroughly after handling chillies as their juices are a severe irritant, particularly to the eyes or tender areas of skin. To remove all pungency, after washing your hands rub in a little oil, then some lemon juice.

Fresh green chillies The long slim fresh green chillies are sold in Indian stores. Some local greengrocers also sell these. Larger supermarkets now sell them as 'finger chillies'. Chillies from the Canary Islands tend to be milder than Indian chillies. Jalapeño and Serrano chillies from Mexico are more easily available from super-markets. Although these are not ideal for Indian cooking, they can be used.

Dried red chillies When fresh green chillies are ripe, they turn a rich red. These are dried to obtain dried red chillies. One cannot be substituted for the other as the flavour, when the chilli is dried, changes completely. Crushed dried chillies are sold in Indian stores. They can be prepared at home in a coffee or spice mill. Super-markets also sell these. Chilli powder is made by grinding dried red chillies.

Bird's eye chillies These are small, pointed and extremely hot. They are often used whole to flavour oil. Long slim ones are milder and are ground with other spices.

CINNAMON (DALCHINI)

One of the oldest spices, cinnamon is obtained from the dried bark of a tropical plant related to the laurel family. It has a warm flavour valued in savoury and sweet dishes.

CLOVES (LAVANG)

Cloves are unripened dried buds of a Southern Asian evergreen tree. They have a strong distinctive flavour and are used both whole and ground. In India, cloves are used as a breath freshener. Clove oil is also used as a remedy for toothache.

189

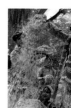

COCONUT (NARIYAL)

Coconut palms grow in abundance in southern India. Fresh coconut is used in both sweet and savoury dishes. In the west, convenient alternatives are desiccated coconut, creamed coconut and coconut milk powder.

CORIANDER, FRESH (HARA DHANIYA)

A much-used herb in Indian cooking, the fresh leaves of the coriander plant are used for flavouring as well as garnishing. They also form the basis of many chutneys and pastes.

CORIANDER, SEED (DHANIYA)

The fruit produced by the mature coriander plant is the seed which is used as a spice. This is one of the most important ingredients in Indian cooking. Its sweet mellow flavour blends very well with vegetables.

CUMIN (JEERA OR ZEERA)

Cumin can be used either whole or ground. It has a distinctive flavour and should be used in measured quantities. The whole seeds are used to flavour the oil before the vegetables are cooked in it. A more rounded flavour is obtained when the seeds are roasted and ground. There are two varieties, black (kala jeera) and white (safed jeera). Each has its own distinct flavour and one cannot be substituted for the other. Black cumin is sometimes confused with caraway.

CURRY LEAVES (KARI PATTA)

Grown extensively in southern India, these have an assertive flavour. They are used to flavour vegetables and pulses. They are sold fresh or dried by Indian shops. Dried ones can be stored in an airtight jar and the fresh ones, which have a better flavour, can be frozen and used when required.

DRIED FENUGREEK (KASOORI METHI)

A strong and aromatic herb, it is native to the Mediterranean region and is cultivated in India and Pakistan. Both the seeds and leaves (fresh and dried) are used in cooking.

FENNEL SEEDS (SAUNF)

These greenish-yellow seeds are slightly larger than cumin, and have a taste similar to anise. They have been used in Indian cooking since ancient times. In India, fennel is used as a breath freshener. The seeds are also chewed to settle an upset stomach.

FENUGREEK SEEDS (METHI DANA)

These tiny, cream-coloured seeds are widely used in vegetable, lentil and some fish dishes. They have a distinctive flavour and, because of their powerful taste, should be used only in minute quantities. They are sold in all Indian stores.

GARAM MASALA

The word 'garam' means heat and 'masala' means the blending of different spices. The main ingredients are cinnamon, cardamom, cloves and black pepper. Other spices are added according to preference. As these four spices are believed to create body heat, they are used to make spiced tea in extreme climates in the Himalayan region.

GARLIC (LASOON)

Fresh garlic is indispensible in Indian cooking. Dried flakes, powder and garlic salt cannot create the same authentic flavour. To yield maximum flavour, it is always used crushed or puréed. Garlic is beneficial in reducing the level of cholesterol in the blood and its antiseptic properties aid the digestive system.

GHEE (CLARIFIED BUTTER)

Ghee has a rich and distinctive flavour and is used liberally in Mogul food. There are two types of ghee, pure butterfat ghee and vegetable ghee. Butterfat ghee is made from unsalted butter and vegetable ghee from vegetable shortening. Ghee can be heated to a high temperature without burning. Both types of ghee are available from Indian stores and larger super-markets. If you wish to make your own, here is what you need to do:

Melt unsalted butter over low heat; allow it to bubble gently and, when it is doing so, you will also hear gentle splattering. This is the moisture in the butter which needs to dry out completely. After a while, the splattering will stop, indicating that the moisture is now removed from the butter. Continue to heat it until the liquid is a clear golden colour and you can see the sediment at the bottom of the pan which will be the milk solids. Once the moisture and the milk solids are removed, the ghee is ready; the process can take up to 45 minutes depending on the quantity of butter you are using. You now need it to cool slightly and strain it into a storage jar through a fine muslin. Ghee can be stored at room temperature. Vegetable ghee can be made the same way using margarine made of vegetable oils.

GINGER (ADRAK)
Fresh root ginger is vital to Indian cooking; dried, powdered ginger cannot produce an authentic flavour. Dry ginger is, however, used in some dishes, though not in curries. Ginger has a warm woody aroma. On the medicinal side, ginger is believed to improve the circulation of blood and reduce acidity in the stomach.

MINT (PUDINA)
Mint is native to Mediterranean and Western Asian countries and is an essential ingredient in Indian cooking. It is easy to grow and also available in most supermarkets. Dried mint, however, is a good substitute.

MUSTARD SEEDS (SARSON OR RAI)
Mustard seeds are an essential ingredient in vegetarian cooking. Out of the three types, black and brown mustard seeds are commonly used and the white ones are reserved for making pickles. Black and brown seeds lend a nutty flavour to the dish. The green leaves are used as a vegetable.

NUTMEG (JAIPHAL)
The nutmeg plant is unique as it produces two fruits in one: nutmeg and mace (javitri). Nutmeg has a hard dark-brown shell with a lacy covering. This covering is mace which is highly aromatic. It is removed from the nutmeg before being sold. The best way to buy nutmeg is whole. Pre-ground nutmeg loses the lovely aromatic flavour quickly. Special nutmeg graters are available with a compartment to store whole nutmeg.

ONION (PYAZ)
This is one of the oldest flavouring ingredients and rarely is any Indian cooking done without it. Brown, red and snow-white onions are grown and used extensively; the use of shallots and spring onions is also quite common.

ONION SEEDS (KALONJI)
These tiny black seeds are not produced by the onion plant. They have been given this name because they have a striking resemblance to the onion seeds. The seeds are used whole for flavouring vegetables and pickles and to flavour Indian breads. They are available in all Indian stores.

PANEER
Paneer is often referred to as cottage cheese in India, but it is quite different from Western cottage cheese. The only cheese that resembles Paneer in taste is ricotta. But, ricotta does not have the texture or cooking qualities of paneer. Paneer is made by separating the whey from the milk solids and is an excellent source of protein. It is unripened and unsalted and can withstand high temperatures while retaining its shape perfectly. Paneer is sold in larger super-

markets. The nearest western cheese I have found is halloumi, but it is salted, so salt quantities in recipes have to be adjusted when it is used instead of paneer.

PAPRIKA

Hungary and Spain produce a mild sweet strain of pepper. Dried and powdered, this is known as paprika. Deghi Mirchi, grown extensively in Kashmir, is the main plant which is used for making Indian paprika. It is a mild chilli pepper which tints dishes with a brilliant red colour without making them hot.

POPPY SEEDS (KHUS KHUS)

The opium poppy, grown mainly in the tropics, produces the best poppy seeds. There are two varieties, white and black, but only white seeds are used in Indian recipes. They are either ground or roasted and ground and give a nutty flavour to sauces while also acting as a thickening agent.

RED LENTILS (MASOOR DHAL)

These can be bought from Indian grocers or from supermarkets.

ROSE WATER

The diluted essence of a special strain of edible rose, the petals of which are used to garnish Mogul dishes. Rose essence is more concentrated and only a few drops are needed if used instead of rose water.

SAFFRON (KESAR)

The saffron crocus grows extensively in Kashmir. Close to 250,000 stamens of this crocus are needed to produce just one pound of saffron. It is a highly concentrated ingredient and only minute quantities are required to flavour any dish.

SESAME SEEDS (TIL)

These pale creamy seeds have a rich and nutty flavour. They are indigenous to India which is the largest exporter of sesame oil to the west. Sprinkled on naan before baking, the seeds are also used with vegetables and some sweet dishes. They are also used to thicken sauces.

TAMARIND (IMLI)

Resembling pea pods at first, tamarind turns dark brown with a thin hard outer shell when ripe. The chocolate-brown flesh is encased in the shell with seeds which have to be removed. The flesh is sold dried which has to be soaked in hot water to yield a pulp. Ready-to-use concentrated tamarind pulp or juice is quick and easy to use. Valued for its distinctive flavour, tamarind is added to vegetables, lentils, peas and chutneys.

TURMERIC (HALDI)

Fresh turmeric rhizomes resemble root ginger, with a beige-brown skin and bright yellow flesh. Fresh turmeric is dried and ground to produce this essential spice, which should be used in carefully measured quantities to prevent a bitter taste.

YELLOW SPLIT PEAS

These are similar in appearance to channa dhal though they vary in taste. They can be cooked just like channa dhal and, therefore, is a good substitute.

YOGURT (DAHI)

In India yogurt is almost always home-made, usually with buffalo milk which is creamier than cow's milk. Bio or live yogurt with a mild taste matches Indian yogurt best.

Index of recipes

Mridula Baljekar

Great Indian Feasts